Puffin Books
Editor: Kaye Webb
Berry's Book of Cunning C

This second book by Roland Be[rry, author of] *How it Works*, turns away from [describing] inventions and concentrates on the cunning contraptions you can make for yourself. You can construct your own locomotion (skate board and sledge), communication (bush telephone), accommodation (tents and dens); create your own relaxation and supply your own recreation with the instructions for making a hammock and a hot air balloon, fishing tackle, a glider, table-top billiards, a kite and various kinds of boats. You may never actually *need* a bull roarer or a hot-air balloon, but it is useful to be able to make them should the need arise, and there are certainly occasions when a magnifying glass or a door closer would be invaluable.

Exotic and complicated as these contraptions sound, they are not difficult to make. Roland Berry provides clear instructions and illustrations, and even suggests how to find alternative materials from which to make them. If you'd like to be a famous inventor and deviser of ingenious gadgets, but feel your experiments might fall flat without a bit of help, *Berry's Book of Cunning Contraptions* is the very book for you!

Roland Berry

Berry's Book of CUNNING CONTRAPTIONS

Puffin Books

Puffin Books
Penguin Books Ltd, Harmondsworth,
Middlesex, England
Penguin Books, 625 Madison Avenue,
New York, New York 10022, U.S.A.
Penguin Books Australia Ltd, Ringwood,
Victoria, Australia
Penguin Books Canada Ltd, 2801 John Street,
Markham, Ontario, Canada L3R 1B4
Penguin Books (N.Z.) Ltd, 182-190 Wairau Road,
Auckland 10, New Zealand

First published by A. & C. Black 1977
Published in Puffin Books 1979

Copyright © A. & C. Black, 1977
All rights reserved

Made and printed in Great Britain by
Richard Clay (The Chaucer Press) Ltd,
Bungay, Suffolk

Except in the United States of America, this book is
sold subject to the condition that it shall not, by
way of trade or otherwise, be lent, re-sold, hired out,
or otherwise circulated without the publisher's prior
consent in any form of binding or cover other than
that in which it is published and without a similar
condition including this condition being imposed on
the subsequent purchaser

Contents

Introduction 7
How to find materials 8
Bike trailer 9
Pram-wheel go-kart 10–11
Sledges 12–13
Skate board 14
Bush telephone 15
Quill pen 15
Tents and dens 16–17
Oven 18
Haybox 19
Rope ladder 20
Hammock 21
Fishing tackle 22–3
Earth kiln 24
Sundial 25
Water clock 26–7
Kite 28
Dragon kite 29
Hot-air balloon 30
Glider 31
Propeller-powered plane 32–3
Matchstick plane 34–5
Match darts and target 36
Table-top billiards 37
Paddle boat 38

Matchbox boat 38
Steam-powered boat 39
Catamaran 40–41
Musical instruments 42
Wooden xylophone 43
Banjo 44
Thumb pianos 45
Knots and plaiting 46
Whipping 47
Whizz bang 48
Paper ball or water grenade 49
Periscope 50
Secret book-box 51
Electro-magnet 52
Leather sucker 53
Leather pouch 53
Cotton-reel tank 54
Propeller car 55
Water-drop magnifying glass 56
Bull roarer 56
Rucksack 57
Weighing machine 58
Door closer 59
Moccasins 60–61
Tie-dying 62–3
Index 64

Introduction

What do you do when you suddenly come across a pair of pram wheels, or a nice big feather, or a sheet of polythene, or any other piece of interesting rubbish? Stop and think awhile: there is usually something useful that you can make it into.

This book will help you while you are thinking. It will give you ideas on how to make musical instruments, moccasins, even electro-magnets, and perhaps you will be able to improve on my designs and make, for example, a better aeroplane than mine. And if you should want to make a bike trailer, or a quill pen, or a kite—that's when you could use pram wheels, a nice big feather and polythene!

How to find materials

When you set out to make things from this book, you may sometimes find that you have more trouble finding the right materials than actually making the thing.

You will usually have most of the materials you need, but there may easily be something which you have not got. This is the moment to sit down and think. If you cannot find the right thing, you can often use something else instead. For example, if you need some canvas to make the hammock on page 21, ask yourself:

1. Is there a piece of canvas in the house that I can use? (Think of likely places such as the attic, cupboards, under the stairs.)
2. Is there a piece of canvas in the garden, shed or garage?
3. Might any of my friends have some, or know where I might find some?
4. Is there anywhere I could go where people might throw away canvas, e.g. waste skips or rubbish dumps? (It may be dirty, but you can always clean it up.) Having got this far, you are probably losing hope of ever finding canvas, so ask yourself:

1. Is it absolutely essential?
2. Does it *have* to be canvas? If you can think of something else like strong netting, tarpaulin or old carpet, go back to number 1 and start again.

Since there are nearly always many different materials you could use for any one job, the instructions do not always say exactly what you should use. Try to make use of whatever you can find. To help, I usually suggest alternatives, and give hints on where you might find them. But the important thing is not to give up. Keep your eyes and ears open. You may not find anything today to make a hammock with, but one of these days you will find a piece of canvas that is just right.

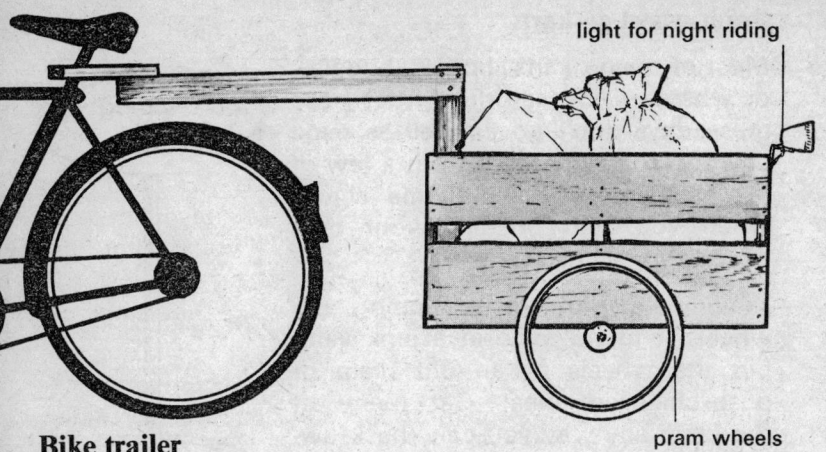

light for night riding

pram wheels

Bike trailer

The basic essentials are a strong wooden box (maybe from the greengrocer) and a pair of wheels. The construction is fairly simple:

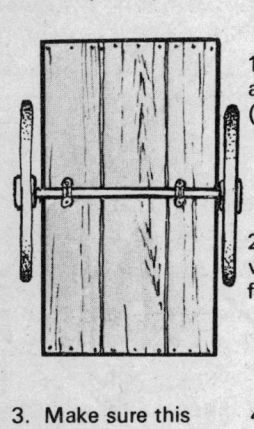

1. Attach the wheels as on the go-kart (page 10).

2. Screw piece of wood firmly to the front of box.

screw

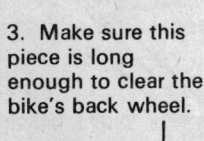

3. Make sure this piece is long enough to clear the bike's back wheel.

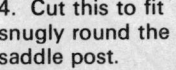

4. Cut this to fit snugly round the saddle post.

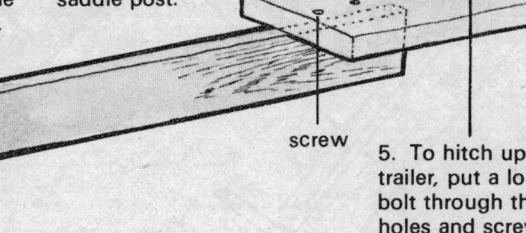

screw

screw

5. To hitch up the trailer, put a long bolt through these holes and screw a nut on the other end.

Pram-wheel go-kart

Most of the go-karts, bogies, buggies, or whatever you call them, that I see these days don't go as well as mine used to, so I'll try to sort out a few of the problems you will come across when you start building your own Grand Prix winner.

Your main problem is finding the wheels. I found mine in a junk yard, but the wheels of an old pram or push-chair are ideal. Get them off the pram any way you can (hacksaw, brute force, etc) but do keep the two wheels and axle in one piece. And don't bend the axle, or your kart will never go straight.

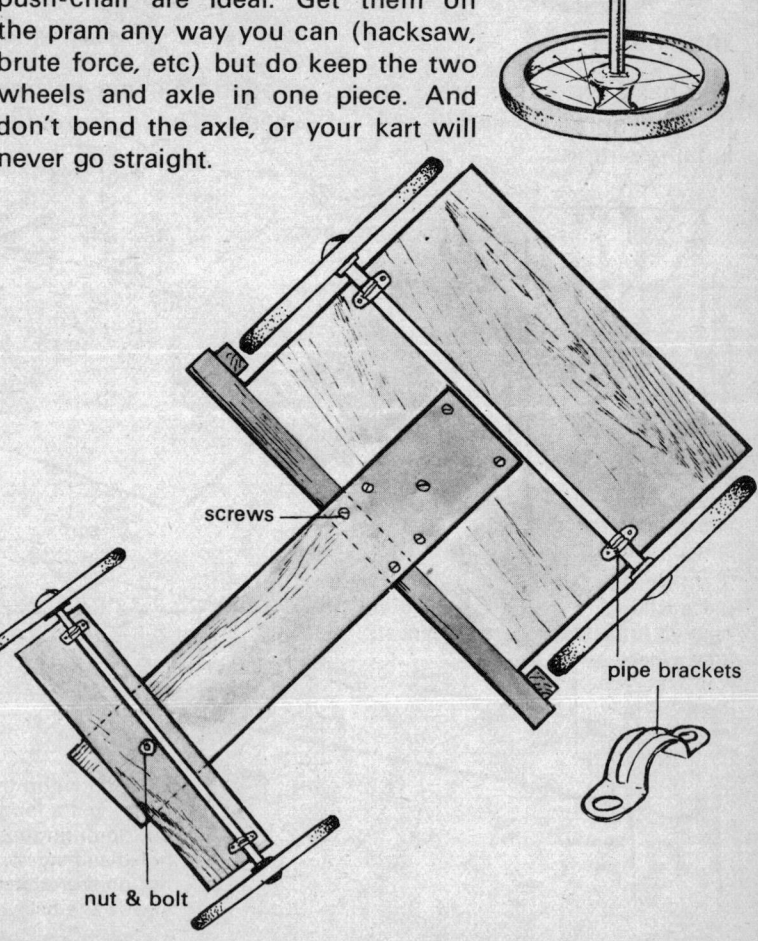

screws

pipe brackets

nut & bolt

1. If your two pairs of wheels are different sizes, put the small ones at the front—it looks better. Use pipe brackets to hold the axles in place.

2. Foam rubber makes a comfortable seat. Canvas or leather-cloth covering looks neat.

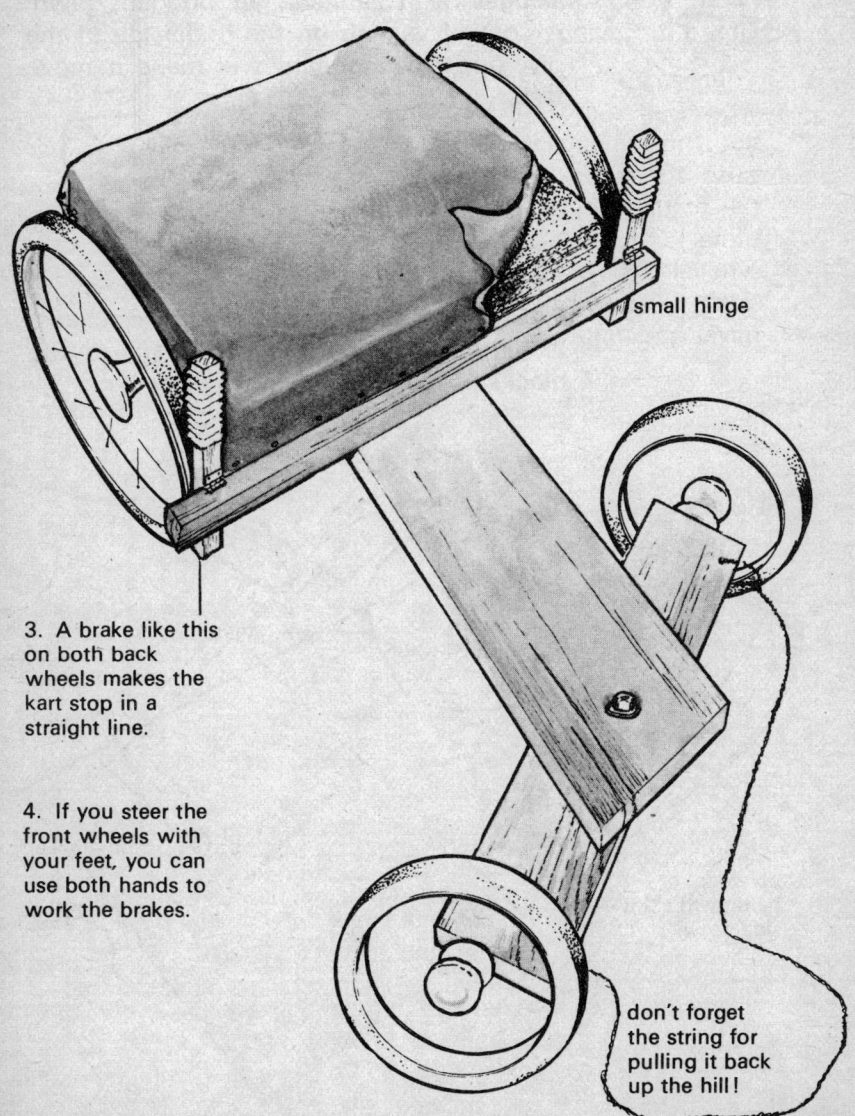

small hinge

3. A brake like this on both back wheels makes the kart stop in a straight line.

4. If you steer the front wheels with your feet, you can use both hands to work the brakes.

don't forget the string for pulling it back up the hill!

Sledge 1

Very often you don't think of making a sledge until the snow is actually falling. This one should only take about an hour to make, provided you can find the materials. It is very good on thin or soft snow, where sledges with runners get bogged down. A coat of varnish on the underside of the plywood or hardboard will make it move faster.

1. Cut out two pieces of wood this shape.
2. Fix the plywood or hardboard to the blocks of wood with screws or nails.

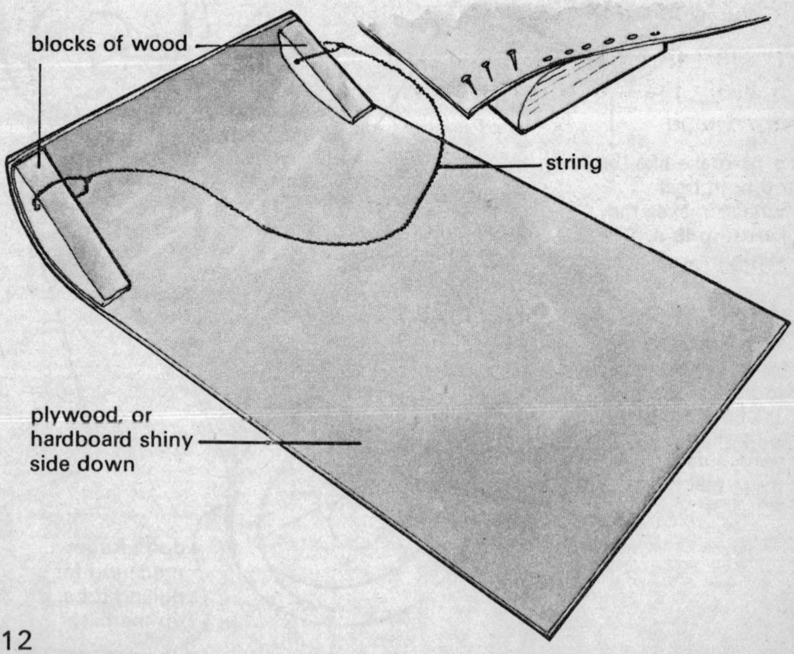

blocks of wood

string

plywood, or hardboard shiny side down

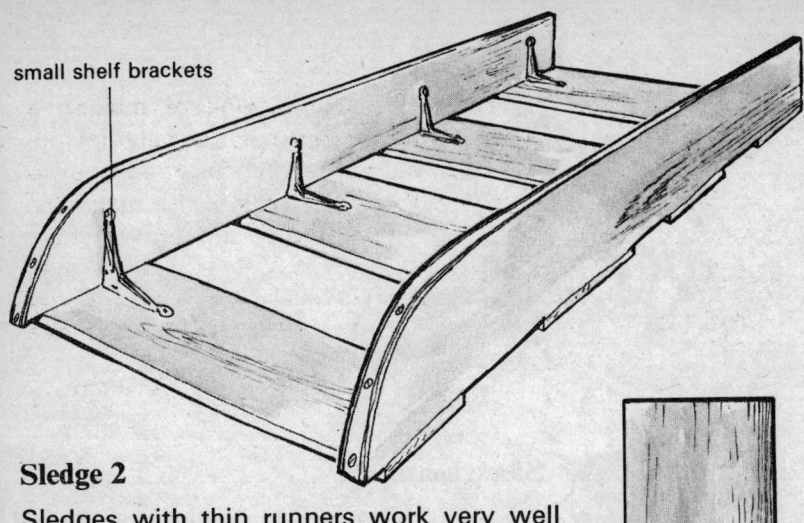

small shelf brackets

Sledge 2

Sledges with thin runners work very well on hard, crunchy snow. I used a sledge like this for three winters; with candle wax rubbed onto the runners it went very fast. The difficult part is finding steel strips to put on the runners. These are essential if you want the sledge to travel fast, but it will work quite well without them.

1. Cut the runners as in the drawing. Smooth them into a curve with sandpaper or a plane.

2. Look around for something to use instead of wooden runners. Maybe an old pram has pieces of metal on it which you could use.

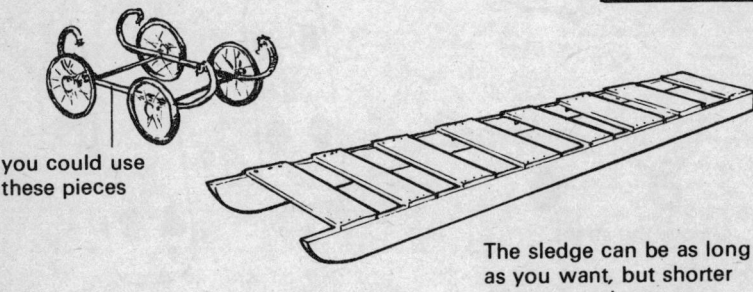

you could use these pieces

The sledge can be as long as you want, but shorter ones are easier to steer.

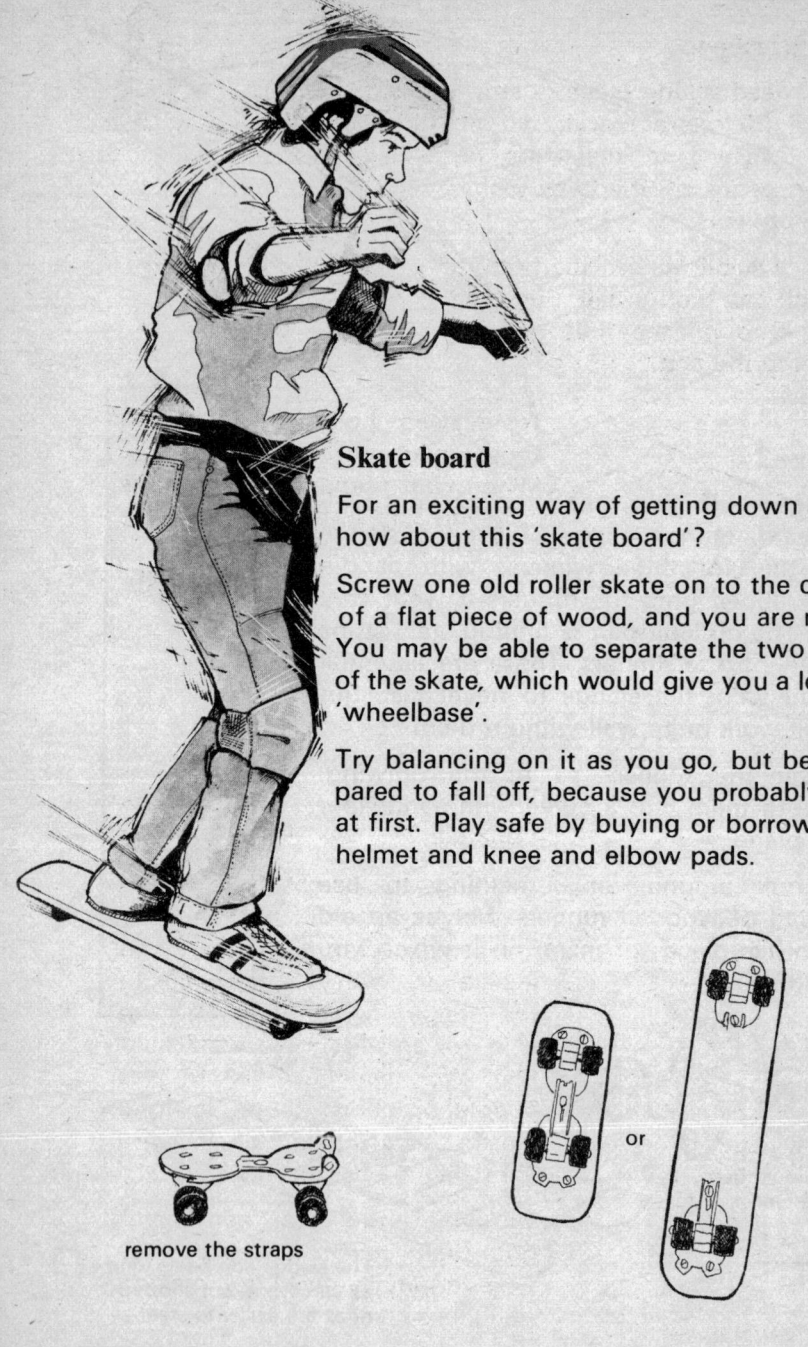

Skate board

For an exciting way of getting down a hill, how about this 'skate board'?

Screw one old roller skate on to the centre of a flat piece of wood, and you are ready. You may be able to separate the two parts of the skate, which would give you a longer 'wheelbase'.

Try balancing on it as you go, but be prepared to fall off, because you probably will at first. Play safe by buying or borrowing a helmet and knee and elbow pads.

remove the straps

or

Bush telephone

You'll need a long piece of string (about 20 metres) and two tin cans. Make sure there are no jagged edges on the cans which could cut you.

Make a small hole in the bottom of each can with a nail. Push the string through the hole and tie a knot in the end.

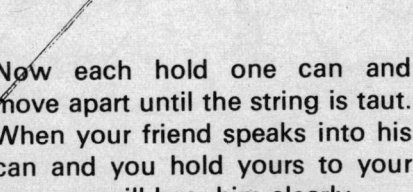

Now each hold one can and move apart until the string is taut. When your friend speaks into his can and you hold yours to your ear, you will hear him clearly.

Quill pen

If you come across a good big feather and can't find any use for it, try making a quill pen. Cut it carefully with a sharp knife to the shape in the drawing. Dip it in ink and it should work as a pen. You may have to cut it a couple of times to get it right. Goose, swan and turkey wing feathers are best for this.

enlargement showing how to cut the end

Did you know that pen-knives got their name because they were originally used for making quill pens?

Tents and dens

I'm sure you have already built at least one den, so I'm only going to give you some tips and maybe a few ideas too. There are many types of tent you can make with a large sheet of canvas, polythene, or even an old carpet:

bivouac   ridge tent

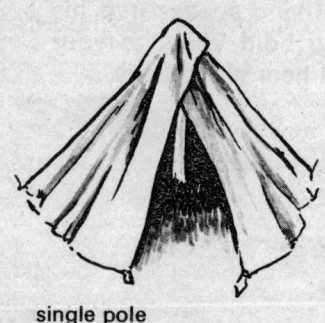

single pole

A more permanent den can be made in all kinds of ways. Look at pictures of primitive dwellings and see if they give you any ideas. A *yurt* (below) is made of a framework of long bendy sticks covered with grass. (You could cover it with cardboard or polythene instead.) A pit dwelling (bottom) has a roof of sticks and grass built over a round pit dug in the ground.

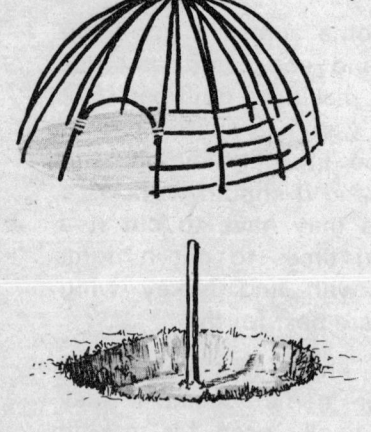

grass covering

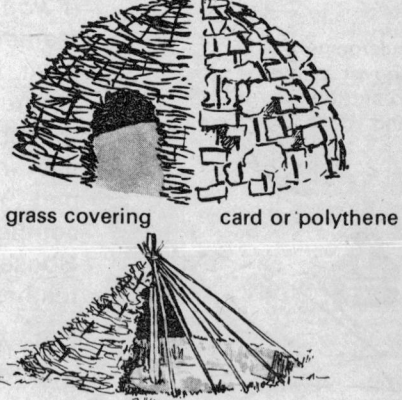

card or polythene

half covered.

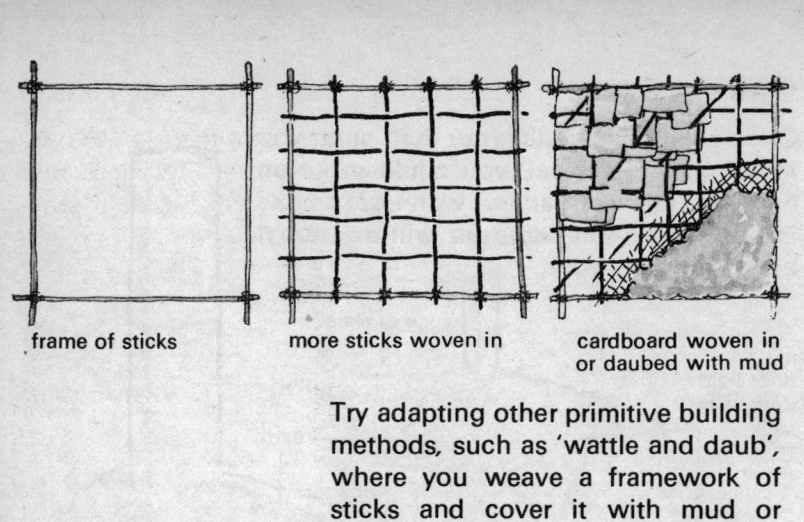

frame of sticks

more sticks woven in

cardboard woven in or daubed with mud

Try adapting other primitive building methods, such as 'wattle and daub', where you weave a framework of sticks and cover it with mud or 'daub'. You could use cardboard instead of mud.

A den nearly always ends up being made of all kinds of different materials from corrugated iron to twigs and long grass—like this:

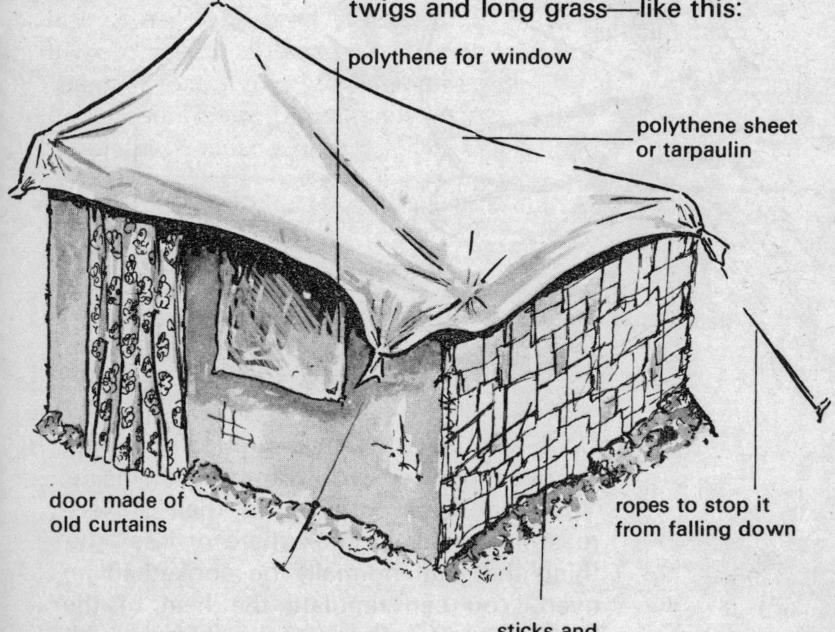

centre pole made of wood or old piping

polythene for window

polythene sheet or tarpaulin

door made of old curtains

ropes to stop it from falling down

the centre pole and corner posts must be stuck firmly into the ground

sticks and woven cardboard

Oven

Once you have built your den and you fancy making a meal, you could make an oven like this, so that you won't get smoke in your food. Any large tin will do, but it must be clean inside.

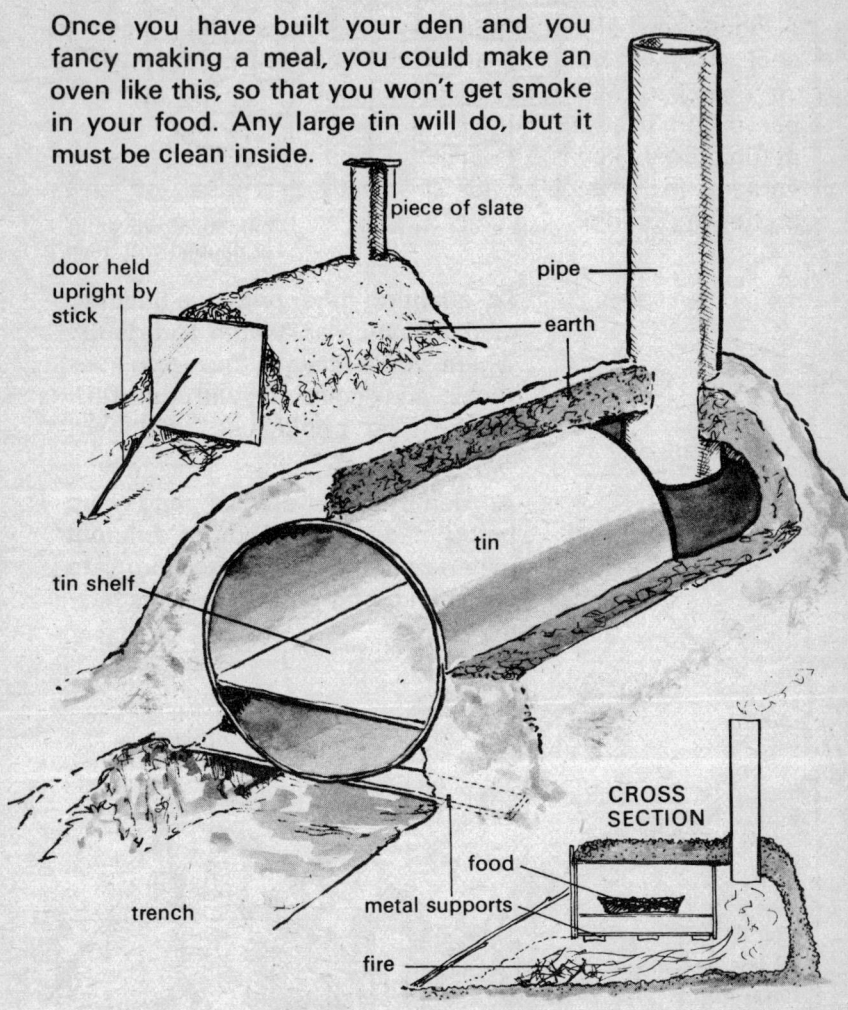

Once you have a small fire going under the oven, put what you want to cook inside. You can bake potatoes in their jackets, roast sausages, or cook more or less anything that can normally be cooked in an oven. You can regulate the heat of the fire by shutting off part of the chimney with a piece of slate or tin.

Haybox

A good way of boiling or stewing things which need to cook slowly is by using a haybox. The idea is this: heat up your food to boiling point over an open fire. Then take the pan off the heat and put it in the haybox. This stops the pan getting cold, keeps the heat in and the food carries on cooking for several hours. This method is ideal for stews and even porridge.

1. Use a tea chest, or even a large hole in the ground, for the hay box. Line it with layers of newspaper.

2. Pack dry grass very tightly round the pan.

3. Put a cushion of dry grass on top of the pan. Cover it with a lid, with a heavy stone to keep it down.

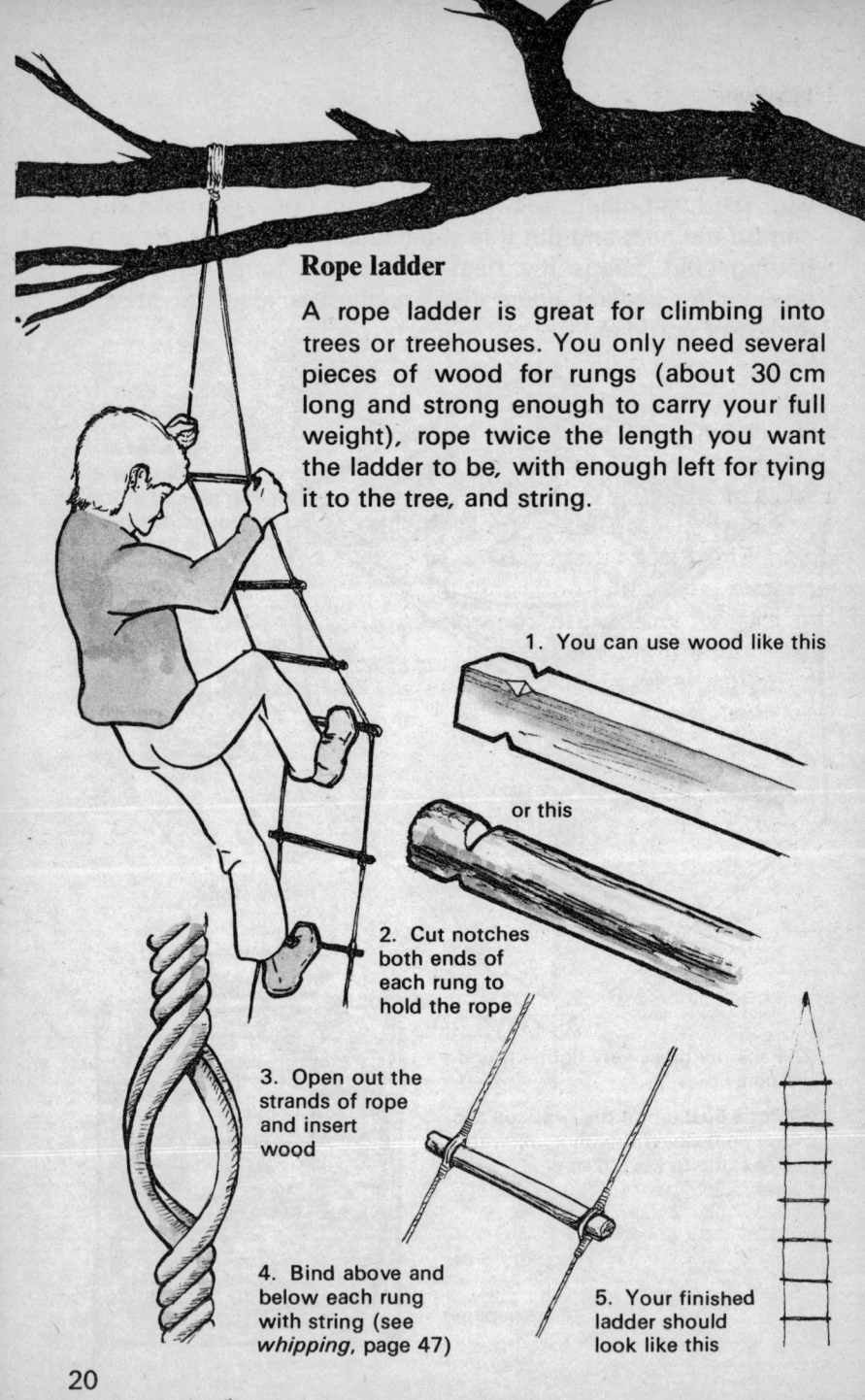

Rope ladder

A rope ladder is great for climbing into trees or treehouses. You only need several pieces of wood for rungs (about 30 cm long and strong enough to carry your full weight), rope twice the length you want the ladder to be, with enough left for tying it to the tree, and string.

1. You can use wood like this

or this

2. Cut notches both ends of each rung to hold the rope

3. Open out the strands of rope and insert wood

4. Bind above and below each rung with string (see *whipping*, page 47)

5. Your finished ladder should look like this

Hammock

You will need: a piece of canvas 2 metres long and about 1 metre wide; two pieces of wood just longer than the width of the canvas; rope and tacks. If you can't find canvas, how about stair carpet or strong blanket?

1. Fold over the edge about 5 cm all the way round, and stitch it firmly.
2. Tack each end to one of the pieces of wood.
3. Turn the wood over and tack again. This makes it strong.
4. Make notches at both ends of the bits of wood. Tie the rope firmly round the notches.
5. String the hammock between two trees.

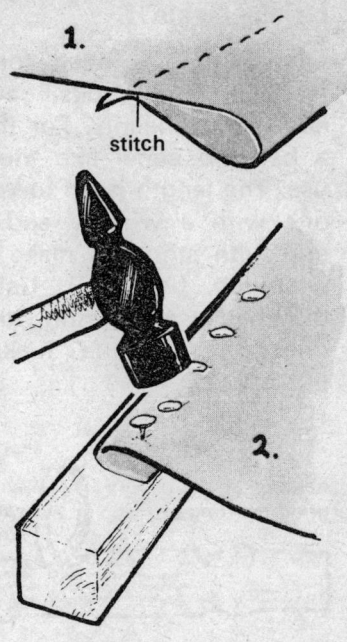

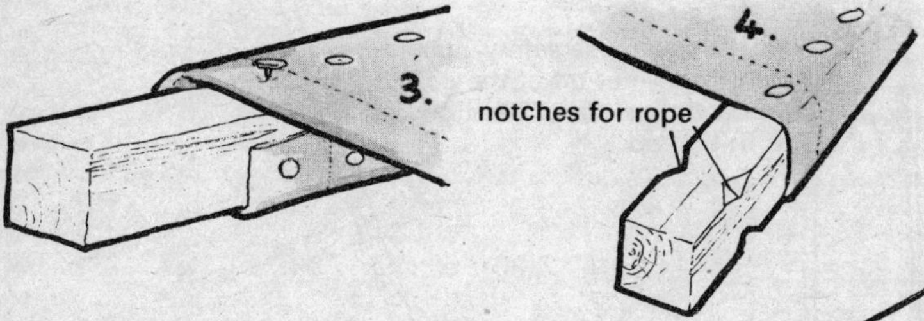

Fishing tackle

Everything you need for fishing, except reel, line and hooks, can be made very easily and cheaply. For the rod itself, use a bamboo cane, like the ones gardeners use. The length is up to you, but try to get one with a whippy end. Bind the thick end with string to make the handle (see *whipping*, page 47). Use wet string for this, because the string then shrinks as it dries on the cane, making the binding tighter.

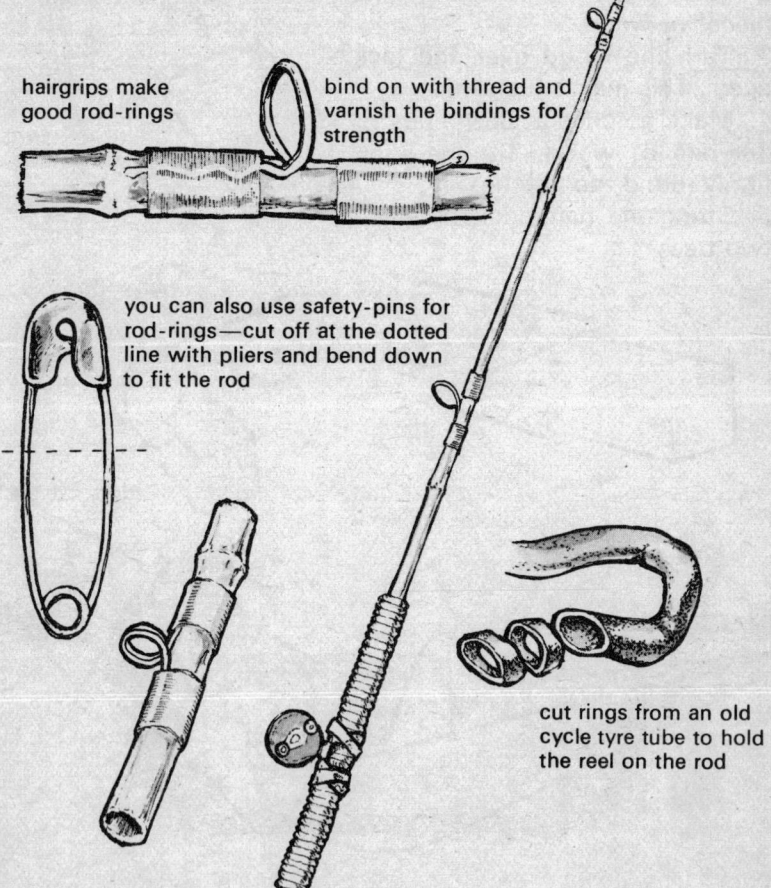

hairgrips make good rod-rings

bind on with thread and varnish the bindings for strength

you can also use safety-pins for rod-rings—cut off at the dotted line with pliers and bend down to fit the rod

cut rings from an old cycle tyre tube to hold the reel on the rod

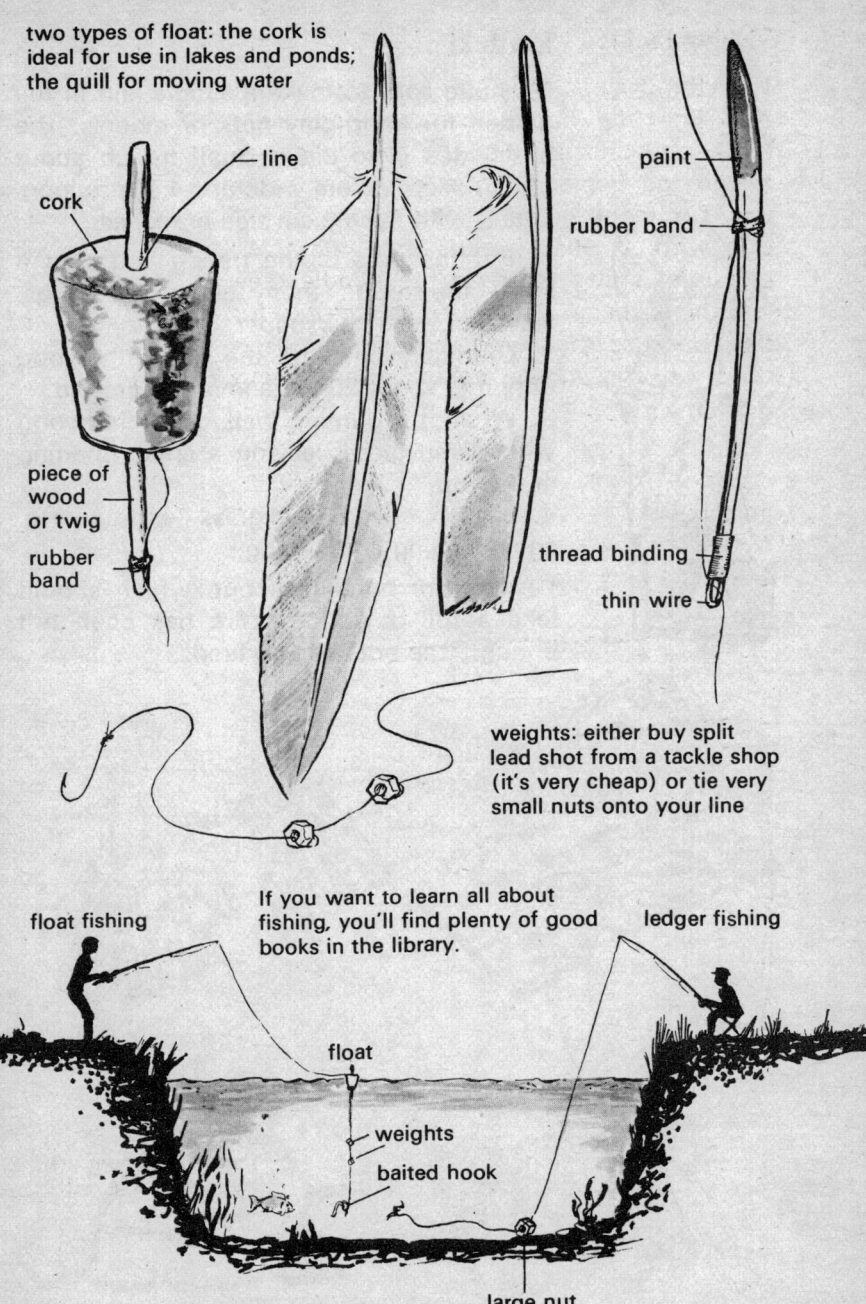

Earth kiln

It's quite easy to make a simple kiln in the garden for firing clay pots or models. The basic idea is to dig a small trench about 30 cm deep, 30 cm wide and 1 metre long. Line it with freshly cut tree branches.

1. Put the pots in the trench and start a small fire round them using dry twigs, leaves or even newspaper.
2. Gradually build up the fire with wood until it is about 20 cm above the ground.
3. When it is burning well, cover the wood with damp grass, leaving a small opening at the top.
4. Lastly, cover the grass with turves, again leaving an opening.

Let the fire burn itself out, which should take a full day. If the fire has been hot enough, the pots will be fired.

Egyptian sun clock

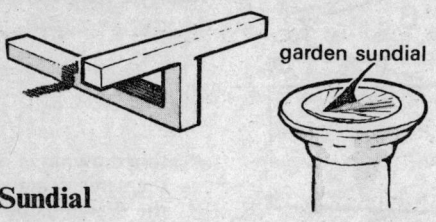
garden sundial

medieval wall sun dial

Sundial

A sundial is one of the oldest devices for telling the time. There are several ways of making a sundial, but setting one up needs a bit of thought. The first thing you need is a pole to throw a shadow when the sun is out. The taller the pole, the more accurate the sundial will be.

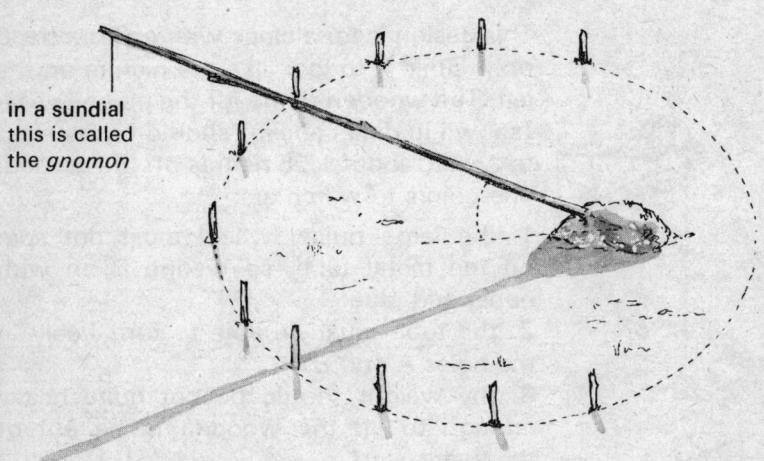

in a sundial this is called the *gnomon*

1. The dial must be on flat ground.

2. The pole must point due north.

3. The angle between the pole and the ground must be the same as your angle of latitude (e.g. London is at 51° latitude, therefore near London a sundial pole must be at an angle of 51° to the ground.)

4. Draw a circle round the pole. Mark on the circle with sticks or stones where the shadow falls at twelve o'clock, one, two etc. (You will have to compare it with another clock at first to do this.) If the circle is big enough, you may have room to mark the minutes as well.

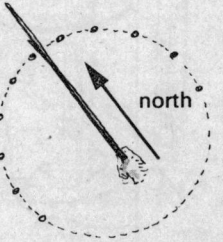
north

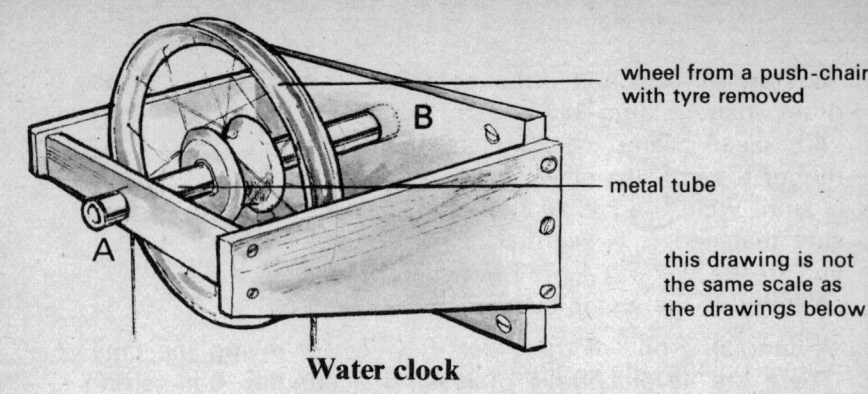

Water clock

This is by far the most difficult thing to make in the whole book. You'll need a lot of patience but it is worth the effort when you finally get it working.

This design is for a clock with an hour hand only. Build it to look like the picture on the left. The wooden frame for the pulley wheel (shown in detail above) should be fastened to a wall, about 1·25 metres off the ground. The points to watch are:

1. the large pulley wheel must not spin on the metal tube, so wedge it on with paper and glue;
2. the tube must be able to turn freely in the holes A and B;
3. the weight should be not quite heavy enough to lift the wooden frame out of the water.

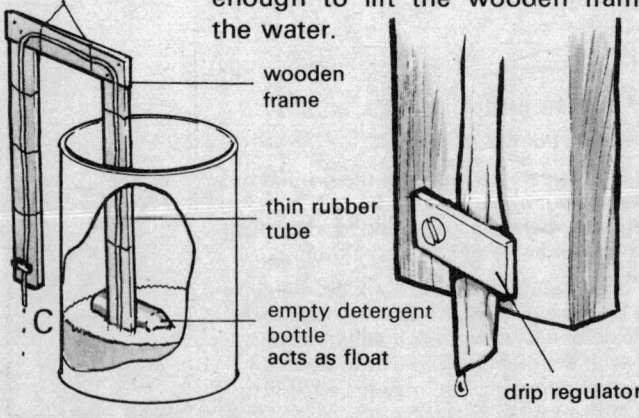

To start the clock, fill the container (oil drum, barrel, large bucket, or whatever) with clean water. Making sure that the rubber tube is also clean, suck on the end C until water begins to come out. (Make sure that end C is slightly lower than the end in the water.) As the water drips out of the tube, the water level in the container drops. The frame sinks slowly with the water, pulling the weight up. This turns the pulley wheel round.

Now fix the hour hand on the metal tube so that it rotates as the pulley wheel turns round.

To make the clock accurate, fix a drip regulator at C. Tightening the screw will make the water run out more slowly, so the clock slows down. Loosening the screw speeds it up.

When the water level gets low, 'wind up' the clock by refilling the water container.

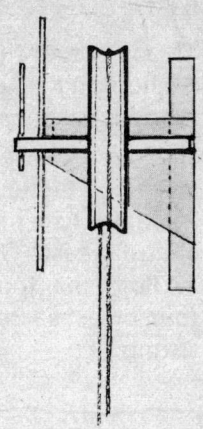

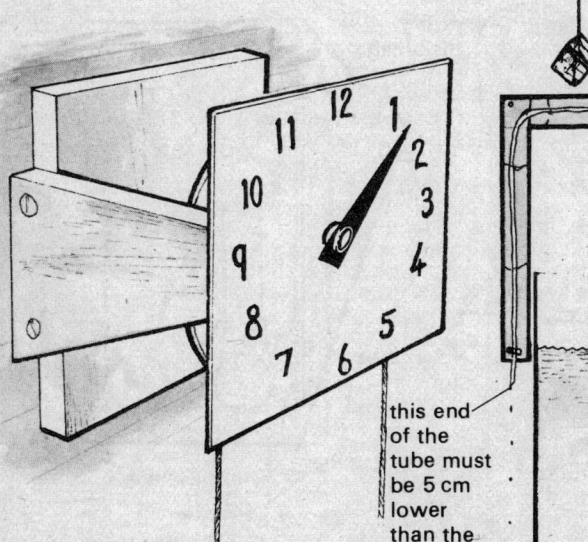

this end of the tube must be 5 cm lower than the other end

Kite

This is one of the simplest kites I have ever come across and it shouldn't take longer than half an hour to make. What's more, it costs next to nothing.

1. Find a metre square of polythene sheet (e.g. bin liner or large polythene bag). Make a crease down the middle.
2. Make two more creases by folding both edges up to the centre crease. Open out again.
3. Fold the four corners in, crease, and cut down these four creases. Put sticky tape on the corners to make them strong.

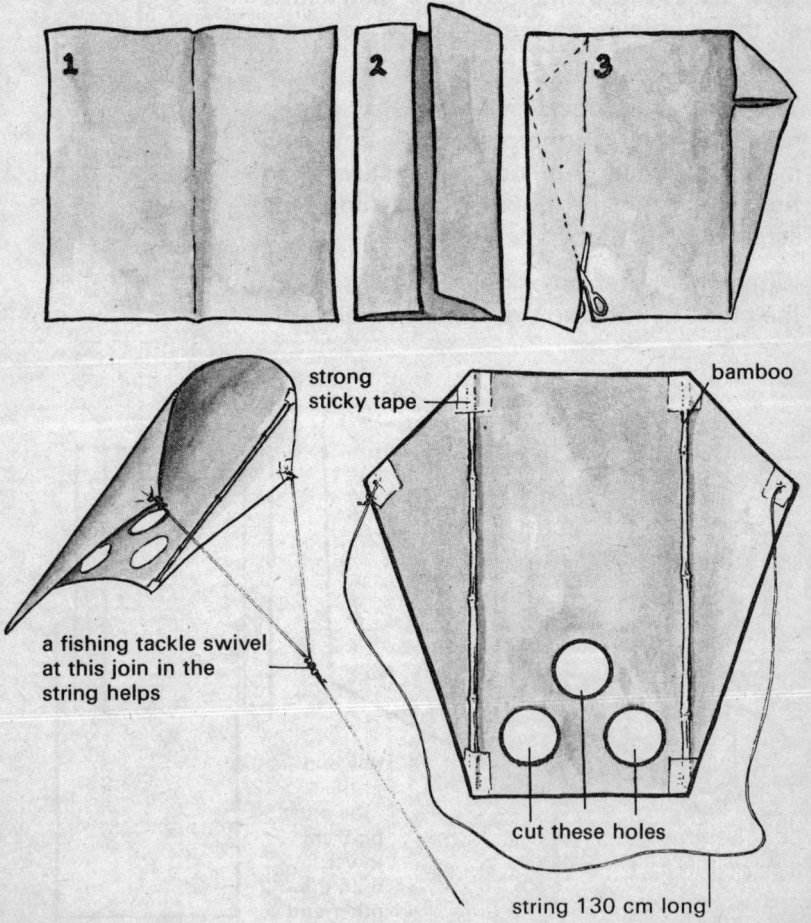

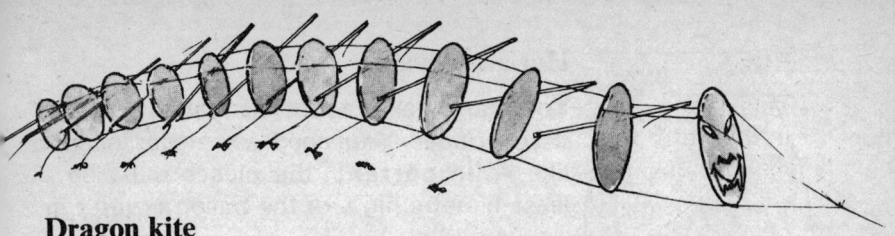

Dragon kite

The dragon kite is a traditional Chinese design and I think it is one of the most beautiful kites in the sky. You can make it as big as you like, but very large ones are difficult to launch. You will need at least eight discs, but add more if you want a longer dragon.

To make the discs, form circles from thin strips of split bamboo or cane which have been soaked overnight to make them bendy. Cover these circles with tissue paper or light polythene.

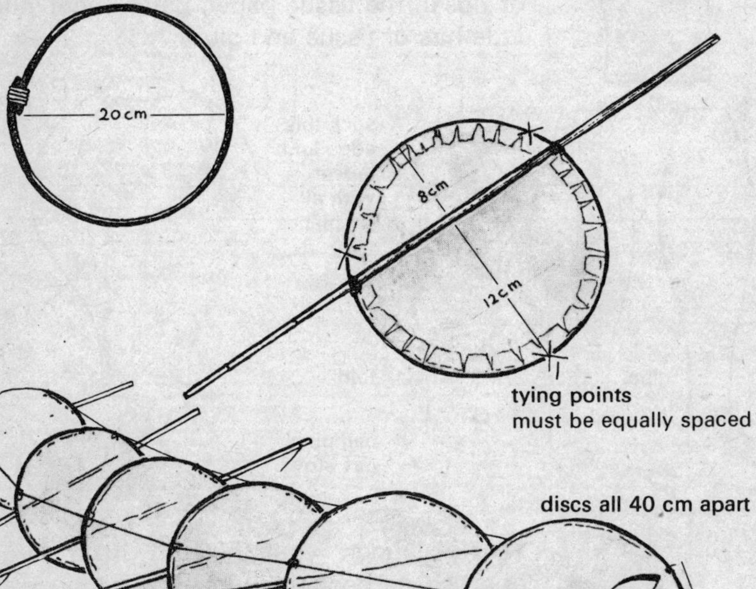

20 cm
8cm
12cm
tying points
must be equally spaced

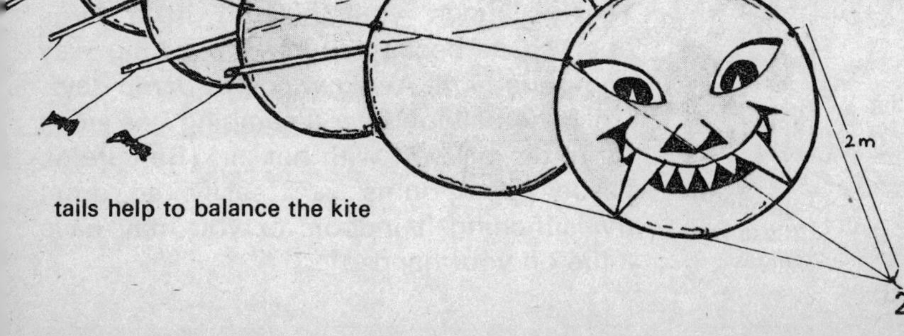

discs all 40 cm apart
2m
tails help to balance the kite

Hot-air balloon

You can make a hot-air balloon out of tissue paper. You need six pieces shaped like A. **Important:** the pieces must be at least 1 metre high, or the balloon won't fly.

Follow the diagrams below: place one section on top of another and glue the right hand edges together with thin paper glue. Fold the top section in half, place another section on top, and glue the next two right hand edges together, and so on. Then glue together the left hand edges of the first and last section. All you need now is a circle of paper, B, to cover the hole at the top. If there are any tiny holes or rips in the tissue paper, patch them with little bits of tissue and glue.

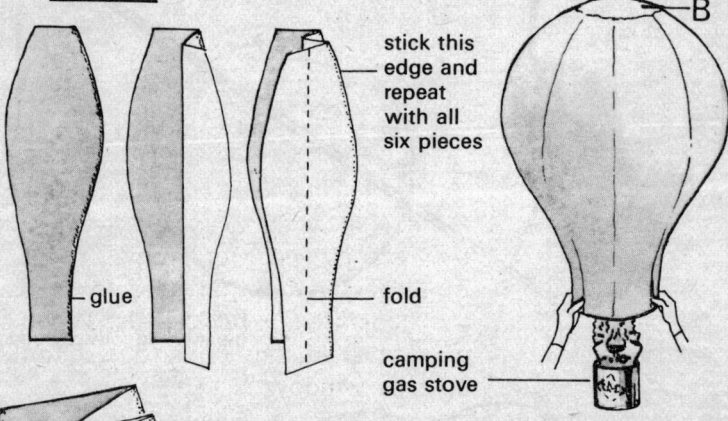

To fly: launch your balloon in a large open space because it may go a long way and quite high. Avoid windy or damp days. Hold the balloon over a camping gas stove to fill the balloon with hot air. (Be careful, tissue paper burns very easily, so don't try launching it indoors or you may have a fire on your hands.)

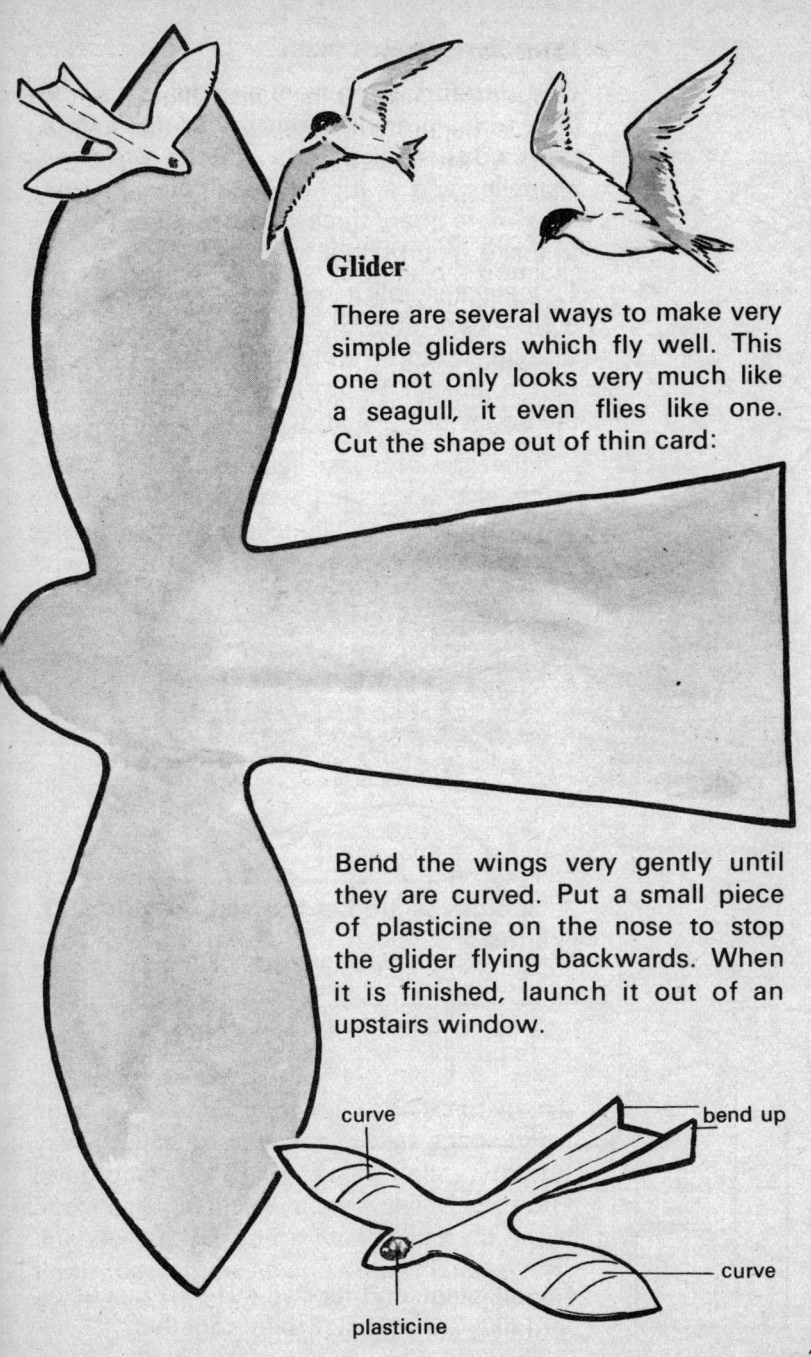

Glider

There are several ways to make very simple gliders which fly well. This one not only looks very much like a seagull, it even flies like one. Cut the shape out of thin card:

Bend the wings very gently until they are curved. Put a small piece of plasticine on the nose to stop the glider flying backwards. When it is finished, launch it out of an upstairs window.

Propeller-powered plane

One step further on from a glider is a plane driven by a propeller. This one is made from thin card (or thick paper), a model aeroplane propeller and a rubber band. It shouldn't take more than three-quarters of an hour to make. You build it like this:

1. Fuselage: roll a piece of card 30 cm × 9 cm into a tube. Glue it up.
2. Wings: cut an oblong of card 40 cm × 19 cm. Fold it 10 cm from one edge. Stick the edges of the card together as shown.

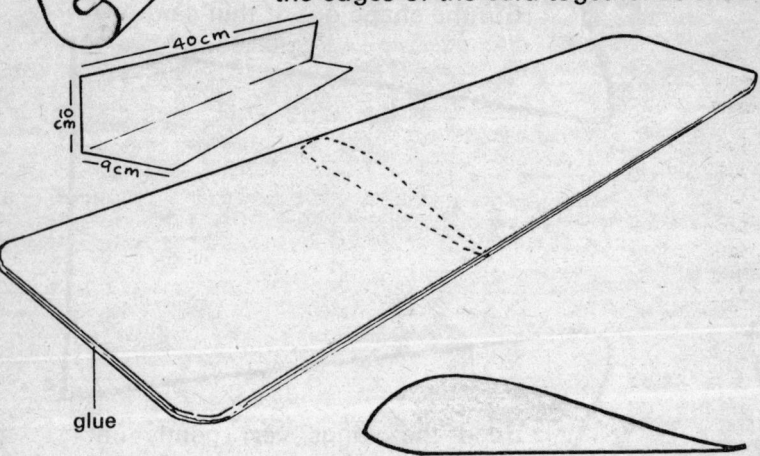

3. A cross section of the wing should look like this.

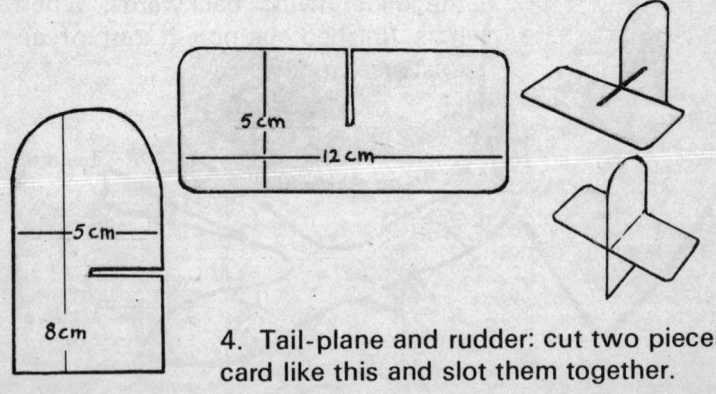

4. Tail-plane and rudder: cut two pieces of card like this and slot them together.

5. This is how the whole plane fits together:

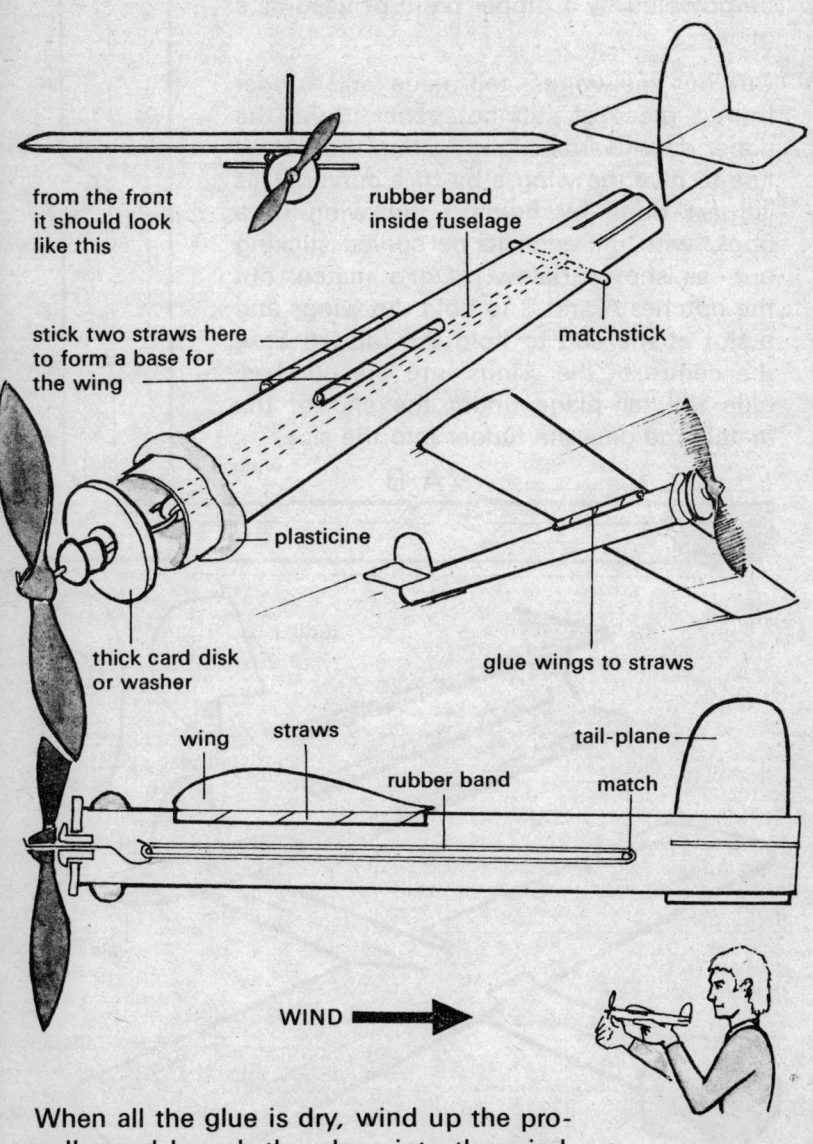

When all the glue is dry, wind up the propeller and launch the plane into the wind. If it dives too fast, take off some of the plasticine.

Matchstick plane

Here is a very small aeroplane which can be powered by a rubber band or used as a glider.

Cut out the wings, tail-plane and rudder from a piece of stiff notepaper. Bend the paper downwards slightly along the dotted line to give the wing a bit of a curve. (This is best done by holding the wing in a book, with the edge to be curved sticking out, as shown below.) On a match, cut the notches A and B to hold the wings and a slot at the end to hold the rudder. Ease the centre of the wings into the notches, glue the tail-plane under the end of the match and glue the rudder into the slot.

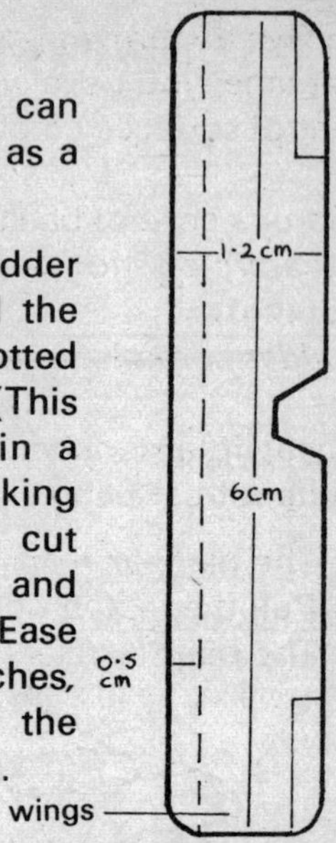

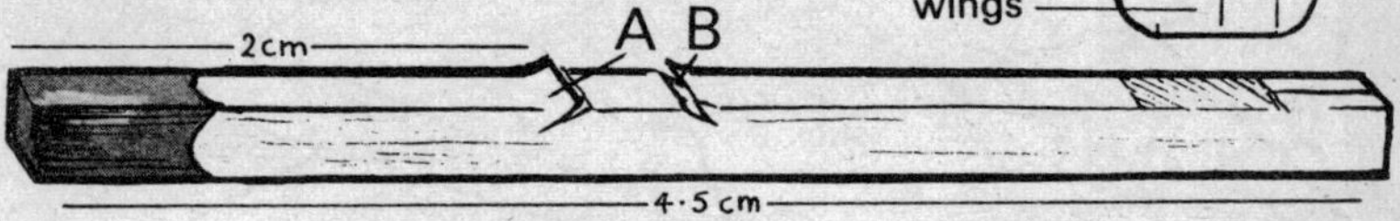

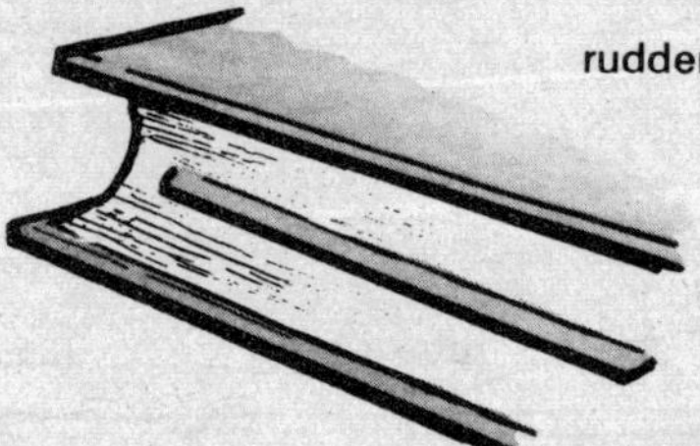

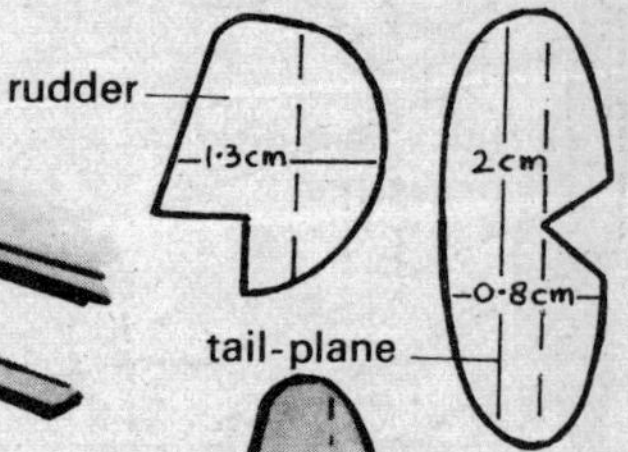

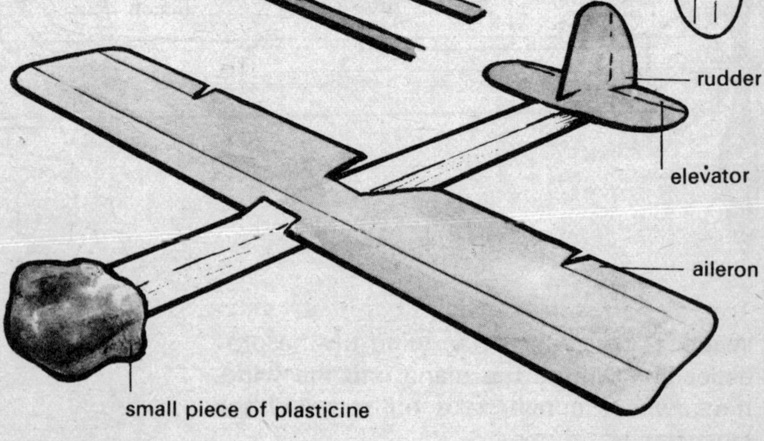

To fly: try throwing the plane. You will be lucky if it flies well first time; you usually have to spend some time adjusting the control surfaces carefully until it works well.

Ailerons control banking left and right.
Elevators control the level of flight (i.e. diving, climbing or looping).
Rudder controls movement to left and right.

A neat little launcher can be made out of a match, a matchbox and a rubber band:

1. The plane is ready to be launched.
2. Pull the match down.
3. The band is released and off goes the plane.

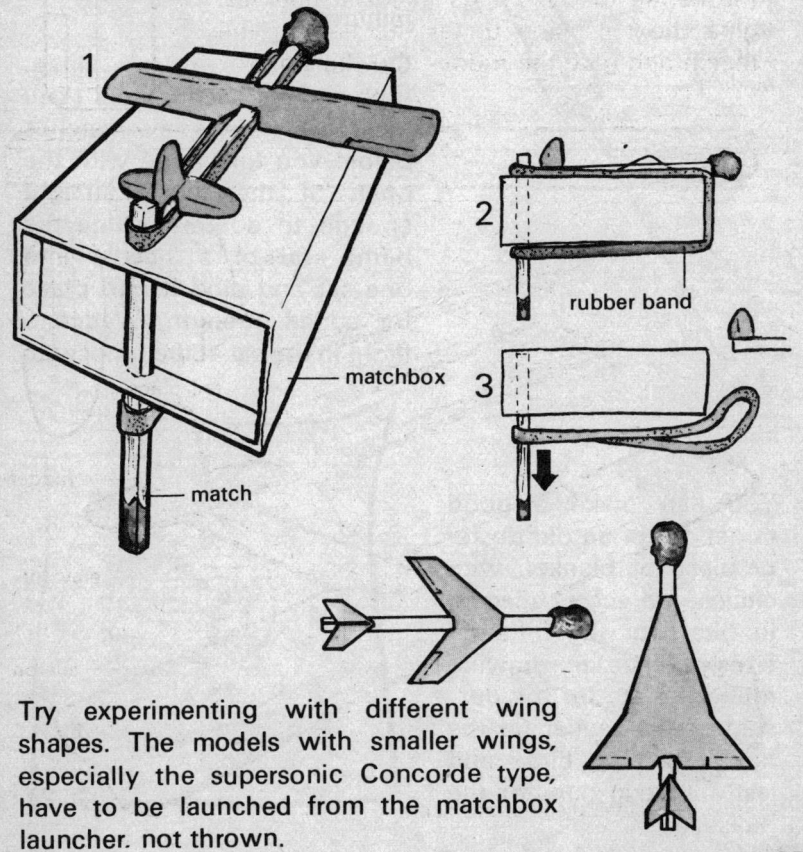

Try experimenting with different wing shapes. The models with smaller wings, especially the supersonic Concorde type, have to be launched from the matchbox launcher, not thrown.

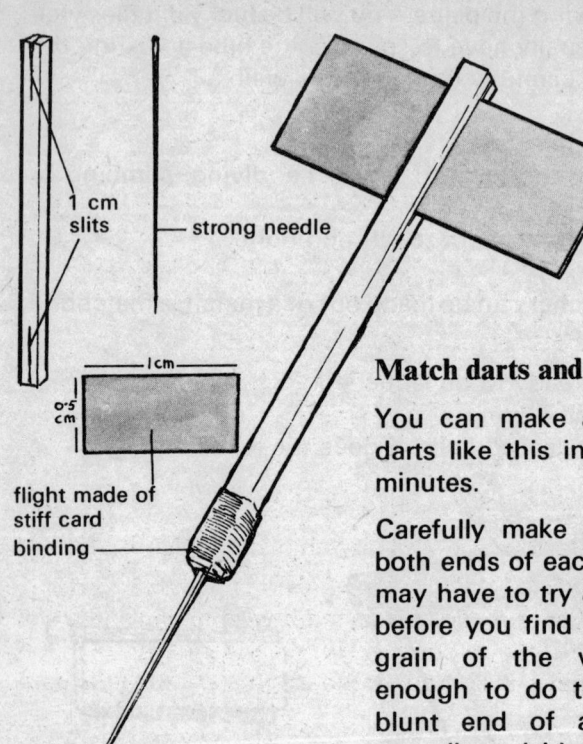

1 cm slits — strong needle

flight made of stiff card binding

Match darts and target

You can make a set of three darts like this in less than ten minutes.

Carefully make a 1 cm slit at both ends of each match. (You may have to try a few matches before you find three with the grain of the wood straight enough to do this.) Glue the blunt end of a needle into one slit and bind it into place for added strength. Wedge a flight in the slit at the other end.

You can make a good target out of an old duster or piece of blanket, with circles and scores marked in biro. For the different sizes of circle, try drawing round a plate for the outside one, a saucer for the next, then a cup, and lastly an egg-cup for the bullseye.

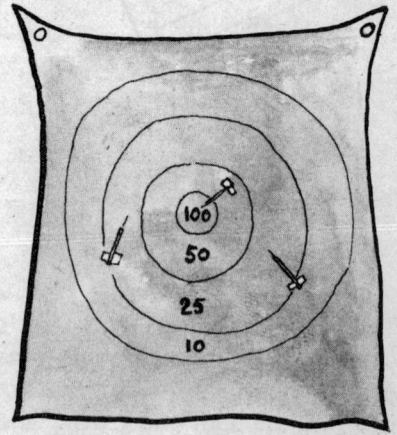

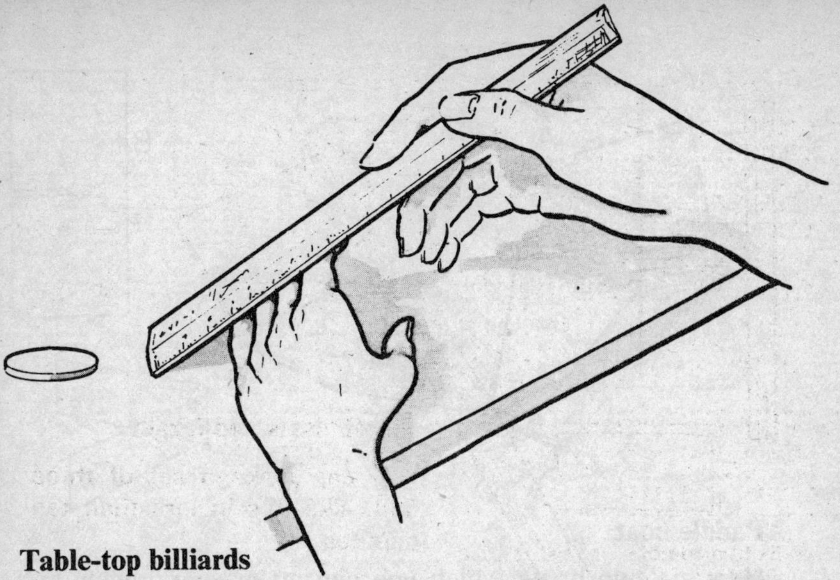

Table-top billiards

Almost any table-top will do for table-top billiards, but it should:

1. be one that you are allowed to mark with chalk;
2. have a smooth, tough surface (formica is ideal);
3. if possible, have a lip round the edge. (If not, you can make one.)

Mark out the table with chalk as below. Use washers or coins instead of balls, and rulers or combs as cues. Play by more or less the same rules as ordinary billiards.

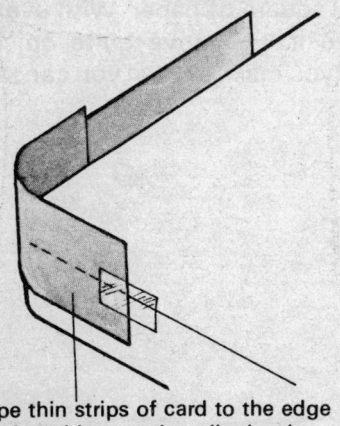

tape thin strips of card to the edge of the table to make a lip, leaving holes for the pockets

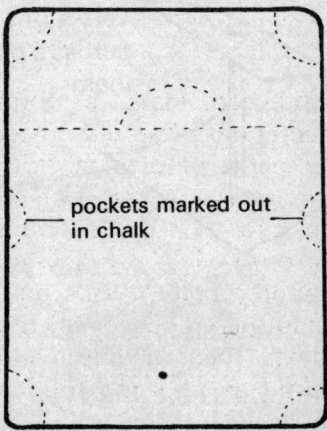

pockets marked out in chalk

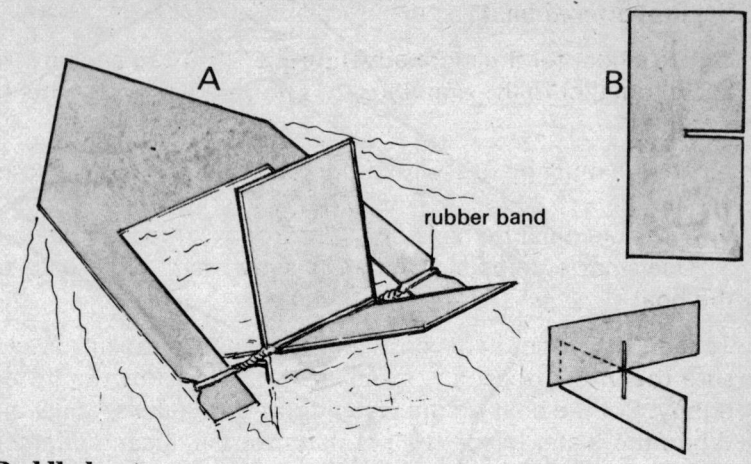

Paddle boat

Here are two boats which you can make very quickly and easily. This one is a paddle boat made of thick card or thin wood. Cut out one piece the shape A for the body of the boat. For the paddles, cut out two pieces the shape B and slot them together at right angles. Fix them to the body with a rubber band and wind it up before putting it on the water.

Matchbox boat

This little boat will take about two minutes to make, using an empty matchbox, a piece of stick and a small square of paper. With even a very light breeze it will move quite quickly across a pond. If you make several you can race them.

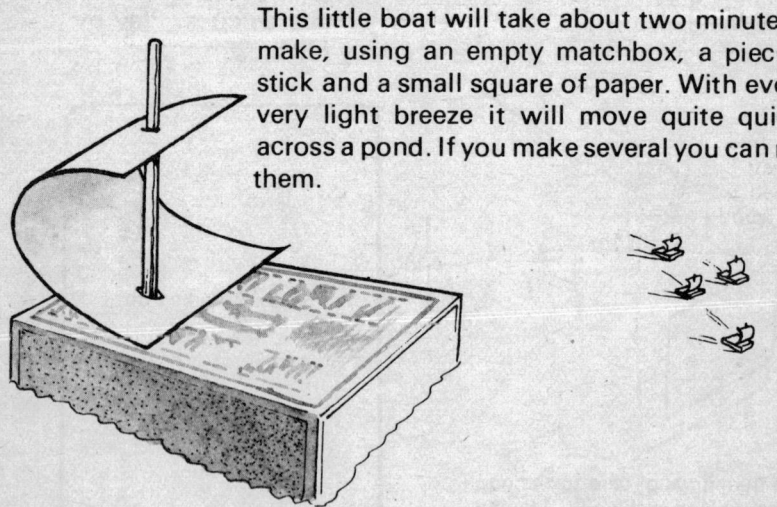

Steam-powered boat

This is a boat for the more adventurous! You can see how to put it together in the drawings, but these are a few points to watch:

1. The tin must be one with a tight-fitting lid, e.g. a syrup or cocoa tin.
2. The hole must be fairly small; make it with a small nail.
3. Use small stumps of candle and glue them to the base of the boat.

To make it go, put half a cup of hot water into the tin. (Make sure the water doesn't run out of the hole.) Put the lid on tightly. Put the boat on the water, light the candles, and wait. When the water inside the tin starts to boil, steam is forced out of the small hole and the boat is propelled forward. It will carry on moving until either the water boils away or the candles go out.

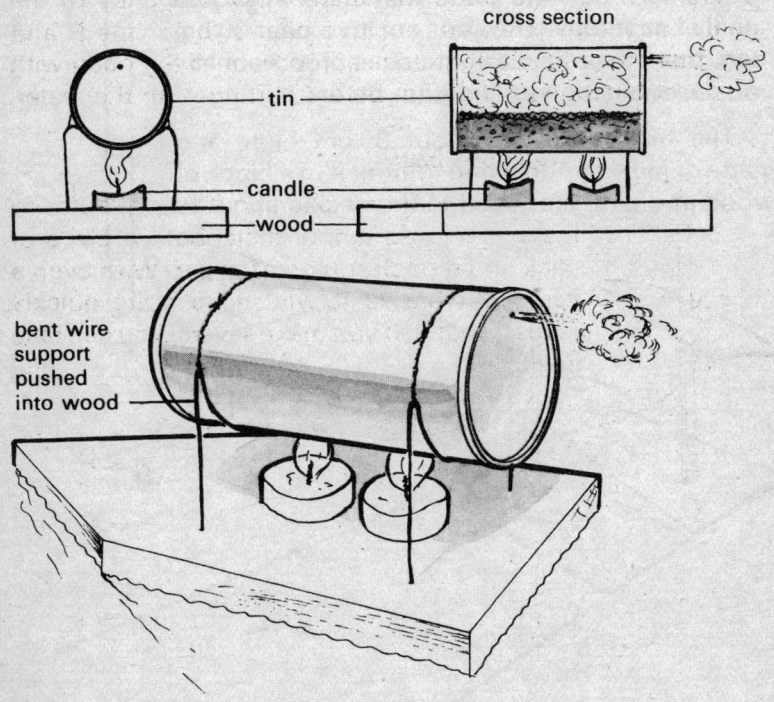

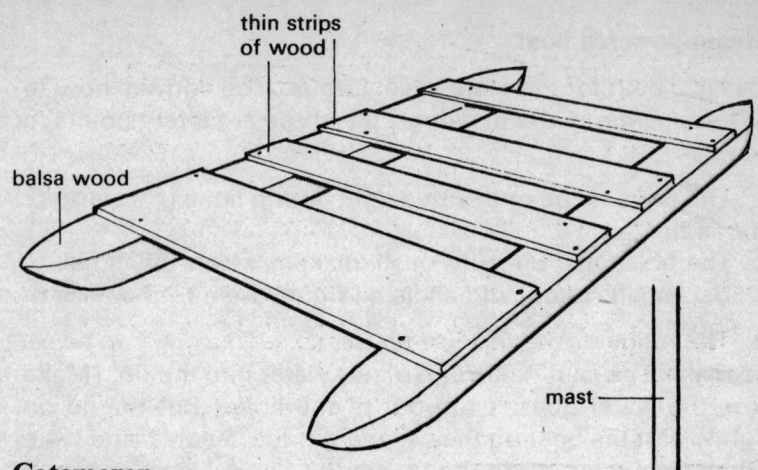

Catamaran

If you would rather use natural wind power to propel your boat, this catamaran should suit you. It is worth spending some time on shaping the twin hulls: if they are made well the boat should handle beautifully. The sizes are for a boat 30 cm long, but if you increase the sizes proportionally you can make one as large as you like.

1. The mast must be about 30 cm high, and made of fairly strong wood. Mount it in a block of wood and glue the wood to the decking.

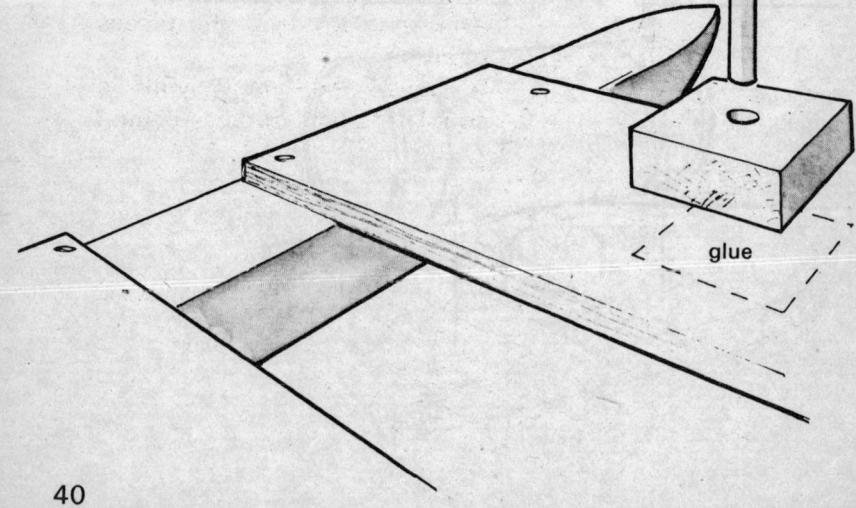

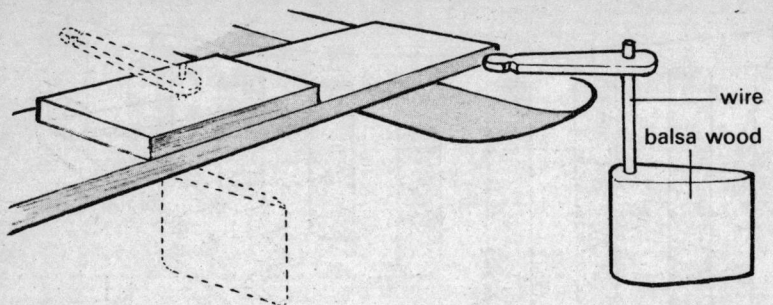

2. The rudder is the trickiest bit to make. This one can be set to any position.

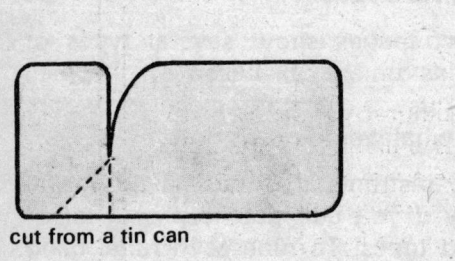

cut from a tin can

3. You could make a very simple rudder from a piece of tin cut out and bent into this shape. Adjust this rudder by simply bending the lower part to the left or right.

4. The cloth sail is hemmed (or even stapled) over the pieces of string.

5. Cover the wood with a couple of coats of gloss paint.

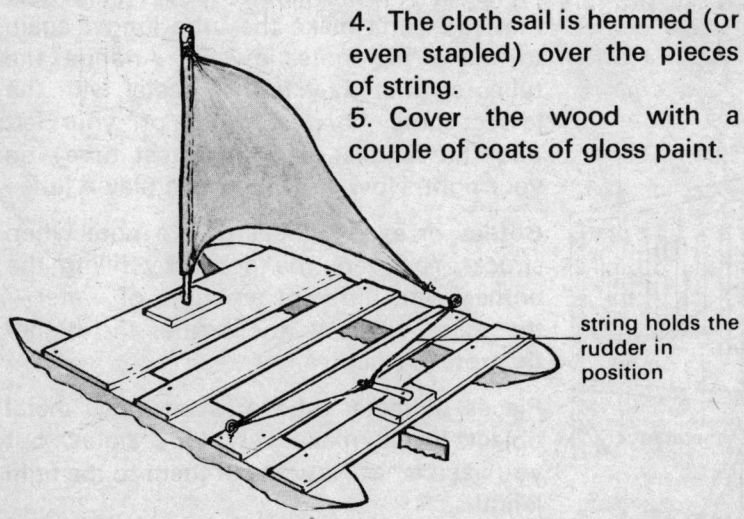

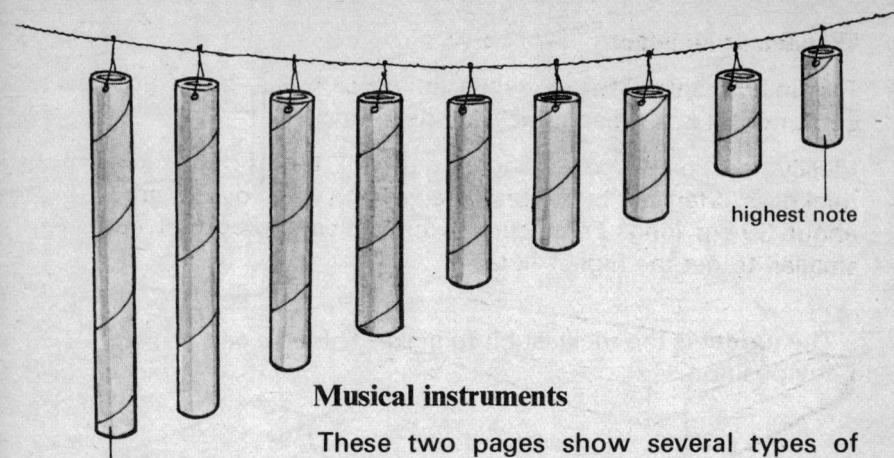

highest note

lowest note

water

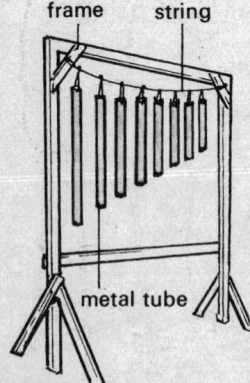

frame   string

metal tube

Musical instruments

These two pages show several types of musical instrument, all based on the idea that you use a separate piece of wood, metal or whatever for each note.

The first instrument is easiest to make, especially if you can get hold of a lot of cardboard tubes. To tune each tube, hang it on a washing line or a piece of wood and tap it gently with a stick. If it makes too low a note, cut a short length off the bottom of the tube and tap it again. The note gets higher as you shorten the tube. (Remember that you can't make the tube longer again to make the note lower!) Arrange the tubes so that they form a scale, with the lowest note (longest tube) on your left and the highest note (shortest tube) on your right. Now see if you can play a tune.

Bottles or even glasses give a note when struck. You vary the notes by filling the bottles with different amounts of water — the more water in the bottle, the higher the note it will give.

Pieces of metal tube or even small metal objects often make very loud notes, but you need a hacksaw to cut them to the right lengths.

Wooden xylophone

This instrument will take a little longer to make, but if you get it right it has a beautiful, delicate sound.

Ideally, the pieces of wood should all be of the same thickness. Start off by cutting the bar for your lowest note about 30 cm long. Then cut the next pieces progressively smaller, to get the higher notes.

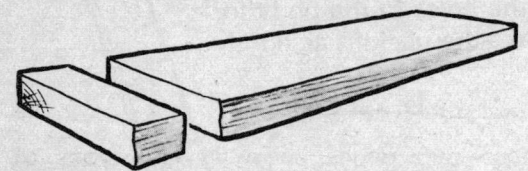

Cut a piece off to make the note higher (as above). Make saw cuts in the wood like this (below) to make the note lower.

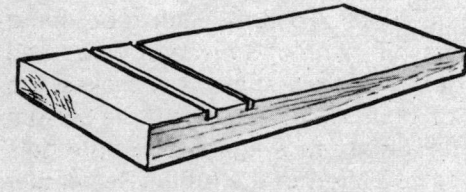

You can make instruments like these from anything which gives a note when struck. The objects must always hang freely, so that they can vibrate and give a note. How about making a 'pieces-of-junk' xylophone?

hang it from a frame, or in a doorway

highest note

lowest note

Banjo

I used to make banjos like this out of wooden cigar boxes, but you don't see many cigar boxes these days. Luckily there are other things which work just as well. (See at the bottom of the page.) Anyway, here are the difficult bits:

1. When you cut the holes in the body for the neck, try to make the neck fit as tightly as possible.

2. The bridge must be stuck flat on the surface of the body. Use wire or nylon fishing line for the strings. Tie them to screws or nails at the bottom of the neck and to eye hooks (for tuning pegs) at the top.

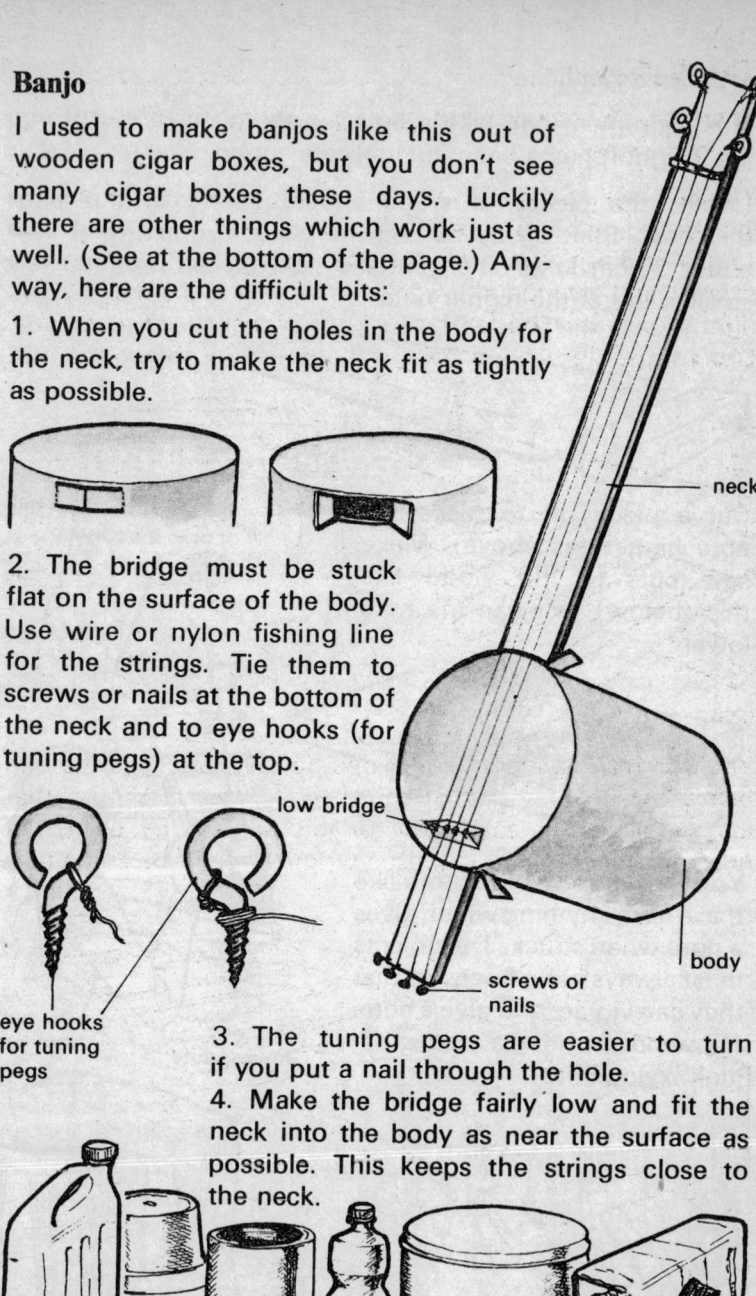

3. The tuning pegs are easier to turn if you put a nail through the hole.

4. Make the bridge fairly low and fit the neck into the body as near the surface as possible. This keeps the strings close to the neck.

Thumb pianos

There are several ways of making a thumb piano, but here are two ideas.

You can make a small one out of a plastic flower pot, lollipop sticks, two pieces of wood, two screws and very strong glue (e.g. Araldite). Tune the lollipop sticks by loosening the screws and moving the sticks in or out until they sound right. Again, the shorter the stick the higher the note it gives. Don't forget to make a hole in the pot to let the sound out.

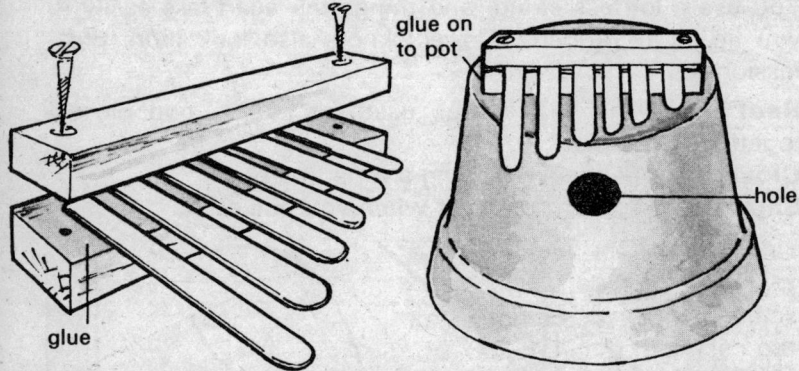

You can make a much bigger one out of a box, like the one below which is made of thin wood. You may find that lollipop sticks are too small for this one, so try using old rulers, combs or anything else you think might be suitable.

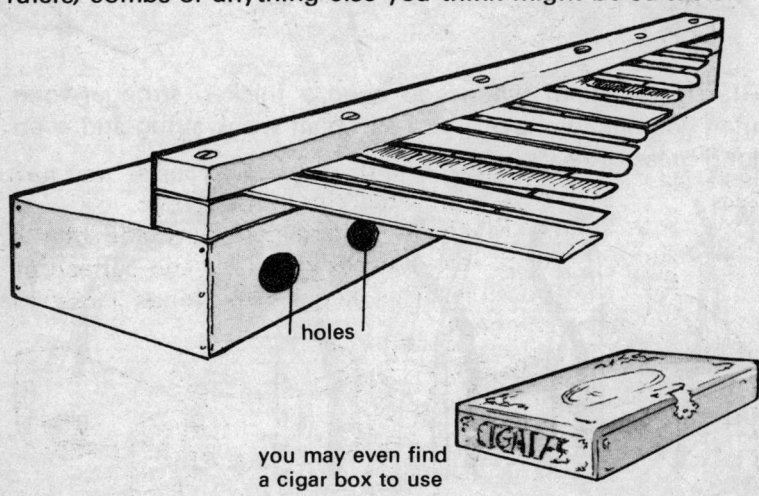

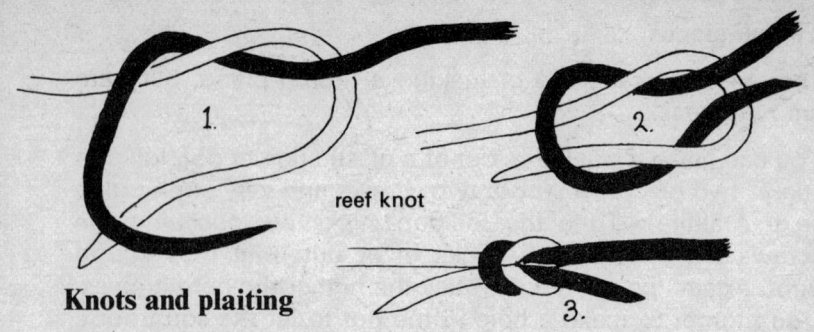

reef knot

Knots and plaiting

You use a lot less string, and things fall apart less easily if you tie knots properly. Correct knots also look more professional.

Reef knot—the old faithful, used for joining two pieces together.
Clove hitch—handy for tying a rope to a post.
Slip knot—tightens on itself when you pull on it.

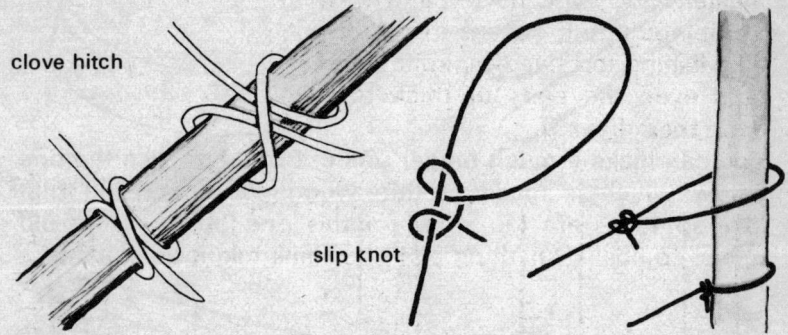

clove hitch

slip knot

Plaiting—useful when you need a thicker, stronger rope than you already have. (You can plait wool, string and even long grass or reeds.)

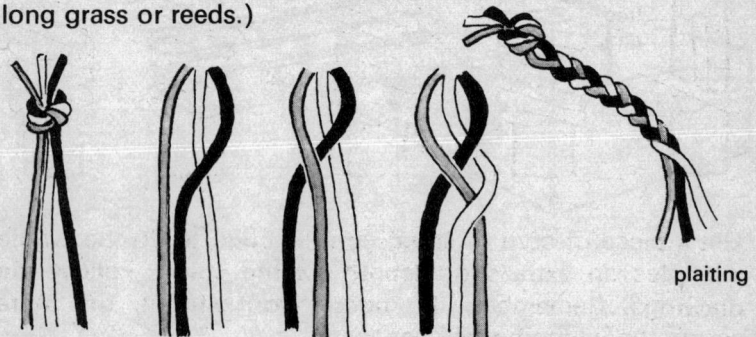

plaiting

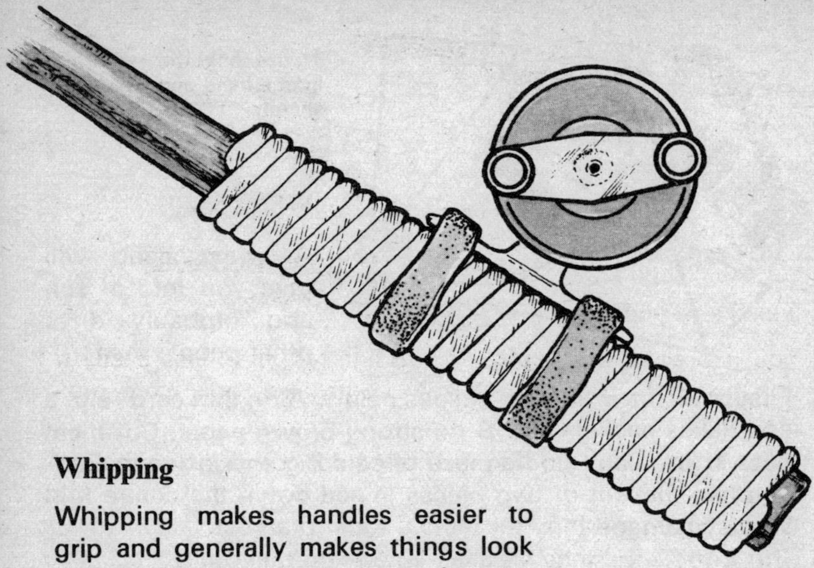

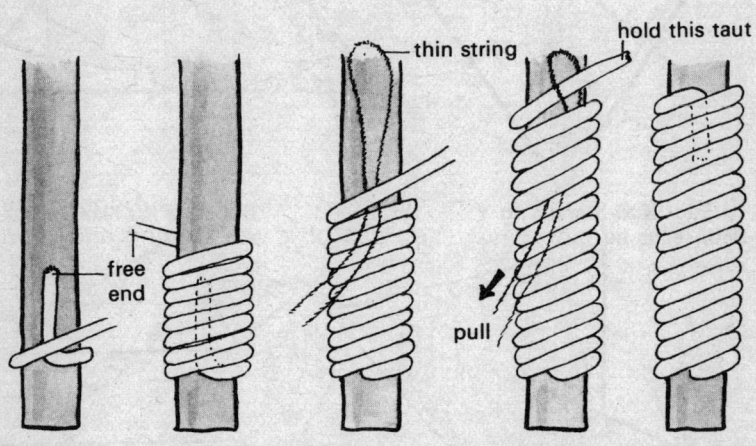

Whipping

Whipping makes handles easier to grip and generally makes things look neater. Once you have learnt how to do it, you'll find dozens of uses for it, like fishing rod handles, knife handles, and even the ends of thick rope to stop them fraying.

Get a piece of cord or string, long enough to do the whole job, plus an extra short length of thin string. Follow the drawings. Remember, the tighter you bind it, the more secure the whipping will be.

To use, hold the end firmly in one hand and flick down sharply.

Whizz bang

A whizz bang will give you lots of fun and probably drive other people mad!

First of all draw the two shapes below, A on thin card (e.g. a cornflakes packet) and B on strong brown paper. Cut them out. (If you can't find a piece of card big enough to make A you can make it of two pieces joined down the centre fold with sticky tape.)

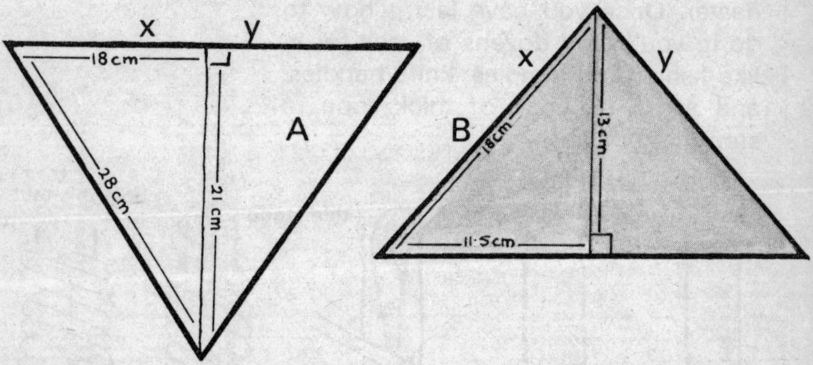

1. Stick X to X and Y to Y with sellotape.

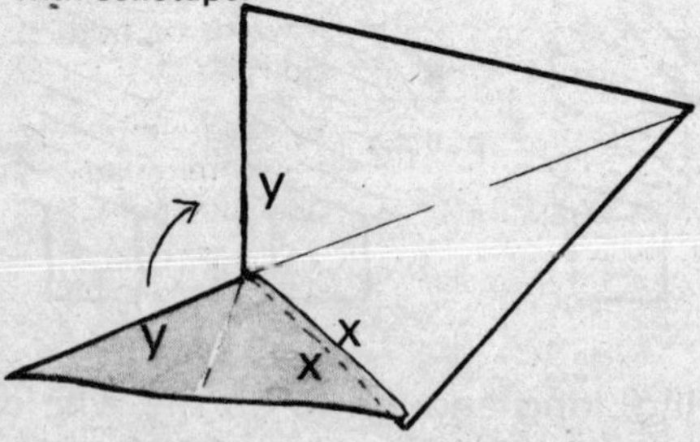

2. Fold it flat like this.

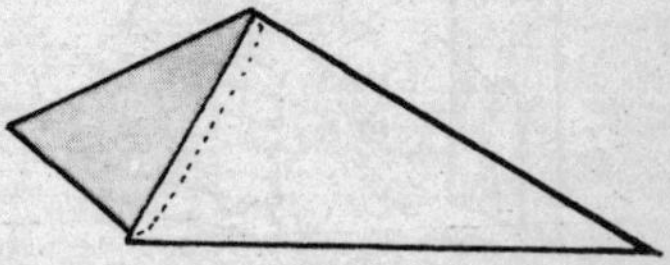

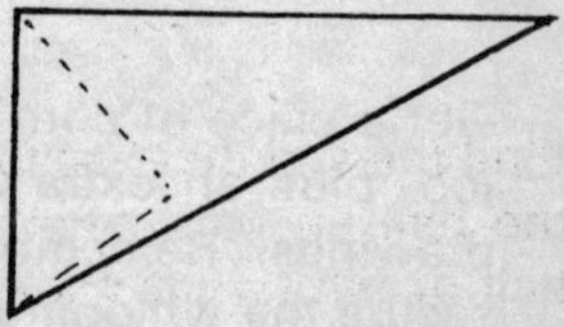

3. Push the brown paper inside the card and fold, and it is finished.

Paper ball or water grenade

This is something I often used to make. You can use it indoors for a nice quiet game of volley ball or outdoors as a water grenade.

All you need is a square of paper—thickish paper if you want to make a ball, thinner paper for a grenade. Follow the drawings, folding along the dotted lines.

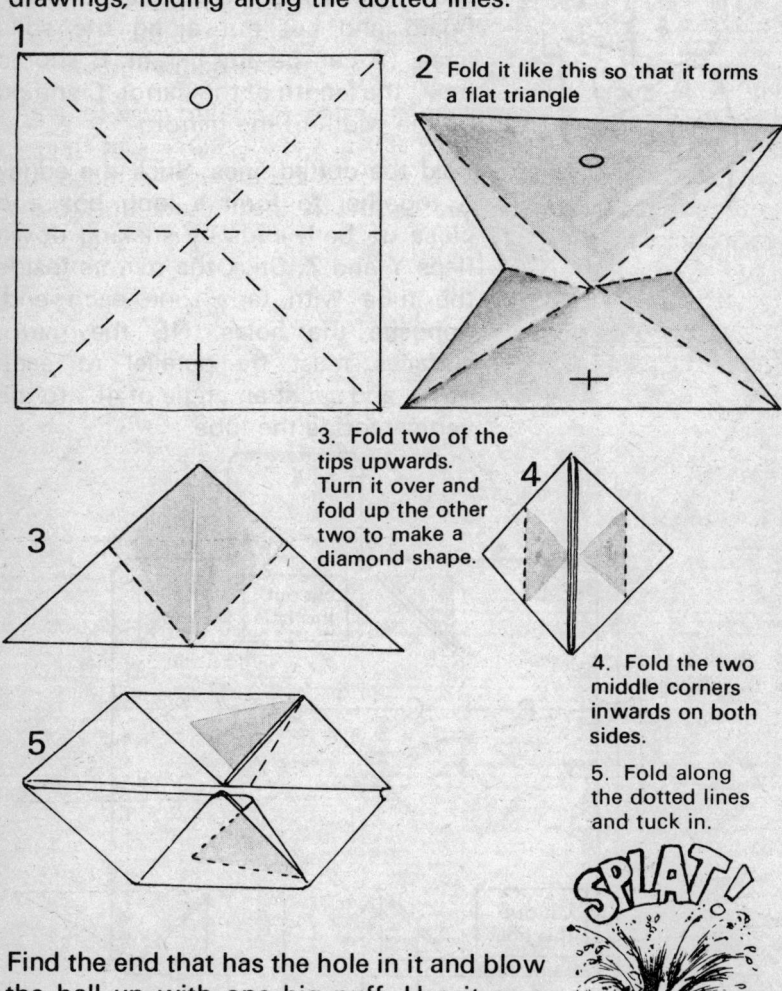

2 Fold it like this so that it forms a flat triangle

3. Fold two of the tips upwards. Turn it over and fold up the other two to make a diamond shape.

4. Fold the two middle corners inwards on both sides.

5. Fold along the dotted lines and tuck in.

Find the end that has the hole in it and blow the ball up with one big puff. Use it as a ball or fill it with water and throw it like a hand grenade.

Periscope

The best material for making a periscope is corrugated cardboard (a big box from the supermarket is just right). You also need two small mirrors of the same size, and sticky tape.

Mark this shape on a flat sheet of cardboard and cut out along the solid lines. (A can be any height. B should be $\frac{7}{10}$ the length of the mirror. C should be the width of the mirror.)

Fold the dotted lines. Stick the edges X together to form a long box and close up both ends by sticking down flaps Y and Z. Stick the mirrors inside the tube with tape, one each end, opposite the holes. NB the mirror surfaces must be parallel to each other, and set at an angle of 45° to the vertical inside the tube.

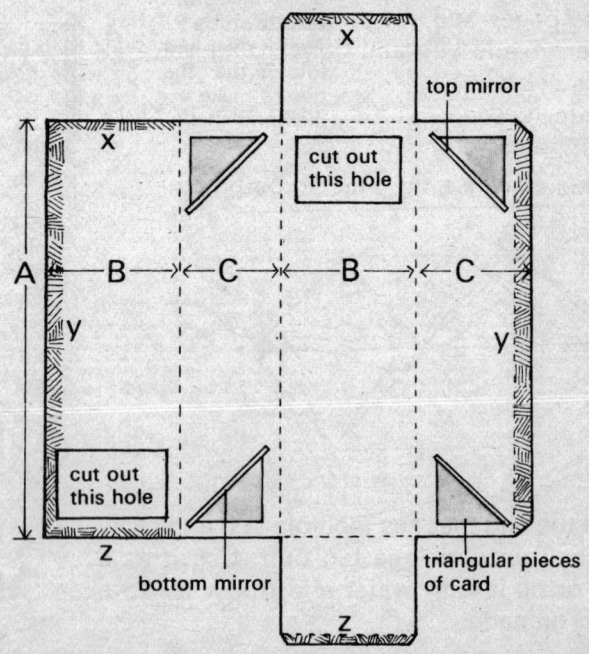

Secret book-box

Find a fairly thick old book that you are sure no-one will want again.

1. Leave a few pages at the front and, on about page 30, mark and cut out a rectangle, leaving the edges of the page uncut.
2. Mark the same rectangle on all the rest of the pages and cut them out. (If you use a sharp blade you can cut through several pages at once.)
3. After cutting, glue together the borders of all the cut pages.

All this takes a long time, so be patient!

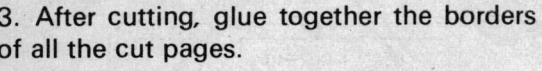

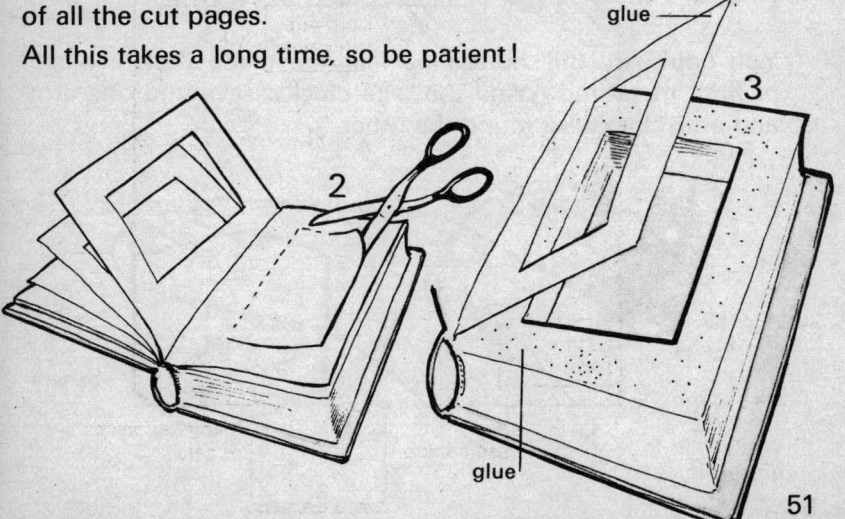

Electro-magnet

An electro-magnet can be very powerful. For the simplest electro-magnet you need a small nut and bolt, about 4 cm long, and some insulated electric wire, such as thin, single-strand electric bell wire.

Neatly wind the wire round the bolt. The thinner the wire, the better it will work, and the more times you wind the wire round the bolt, the more powerful the magnet will be. Connect the two ends of the wire to a battery and then try lifting nails and things with it

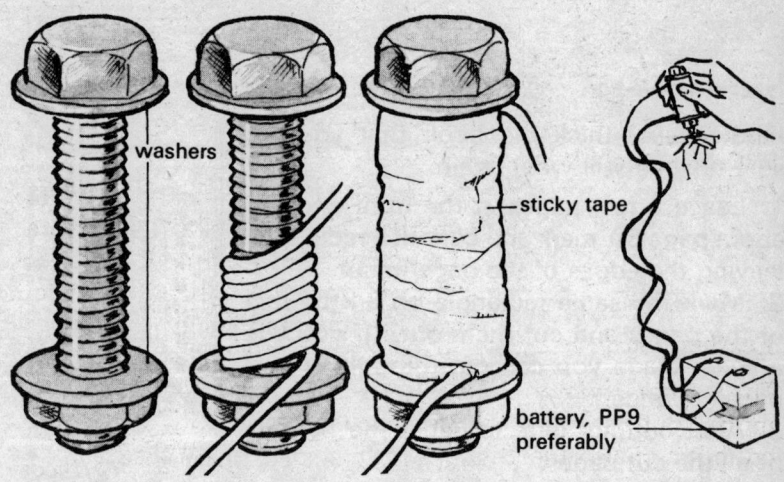

You could try this horseshoe magnet, made from a piece of bent metal rod. Wind the wire clockwise round one arm and anti-clockwise round the other.

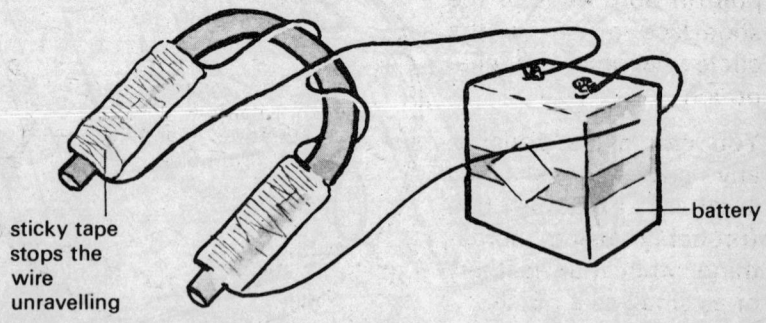

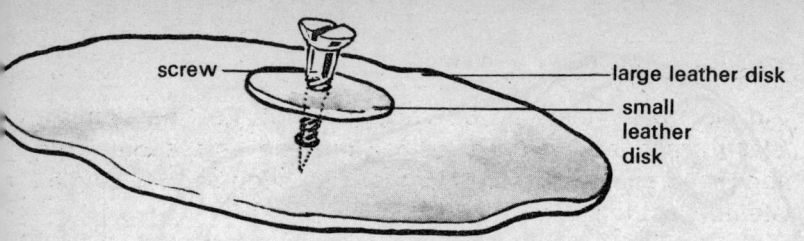

Leather sucker

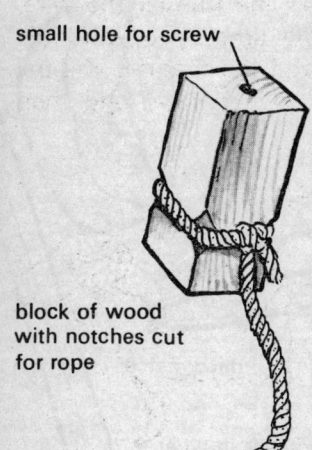

If you happen to have some scraps of leather around, here are two things you can make. This leather sucker will lift fairly large objects, like rocks and boxes. The larger you can cut the circle of leather, the bigger the things you will be able to lift. Screw the leather disc on to a small block of wood, as shown.

To use it, soak the leather in water and then place it on a flat surface of the thing you want to lift. Press or stamp it down as flat as possible. Hold the rope and lift.

Leather pouch

The other thing is a money pouch. Again you cut out a circle of leather, but this time make holes evenly spaced round the edge and thread them with string. When you pull on both ends of the shoe-lace or string, the circle becomes a neat pouch.

You can make pouches any size you like—as large as a duffle bag (probably using something other than leather) or as small as a purse.

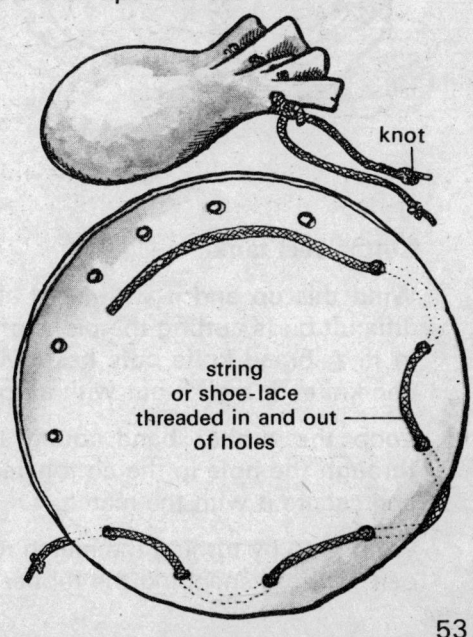

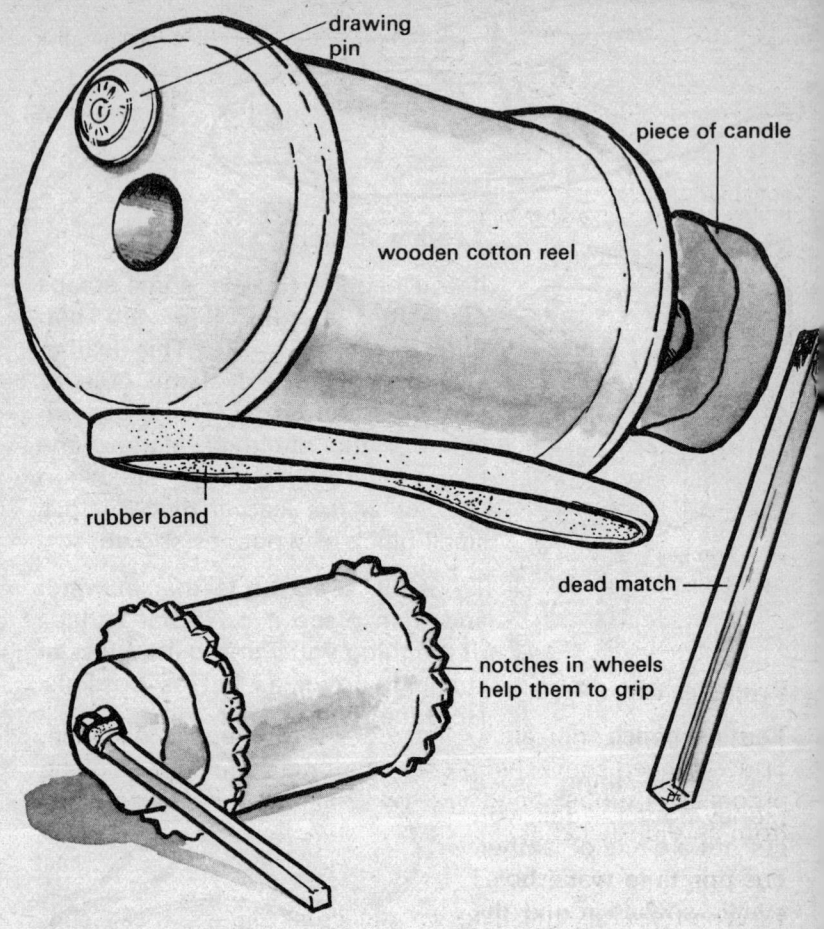

Cotton-reel tank

Wind this up and it will crawl along the ground. The only difficult bit is cutting the piece of candle and making a hole in it. A bread knife cuts best. Make the hole with a small pen knife, or melt it out with a hot knitting needle.

Loop the rubber band round the drawing pin; push it through the hole in the cotton-reel and the piece of candle, and secure it with the match.

Wind it up by turning the match round as many times as you can, without snapping the rubber band.

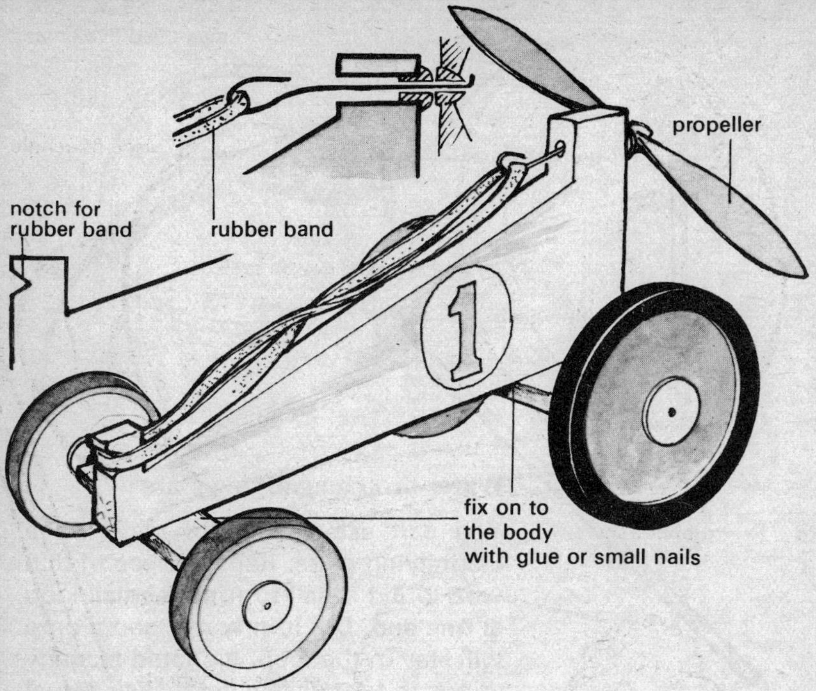

Propeller car

This car will zoom along flat ground for quite a distance. You will need some thin pieces of wood, a model aeroplane propeller, a rubber band and two pairs of wheels on axles from an old toy car.

The points to watch are:

1. When you fix the axles to the cross pieces, make sure the wheels can turn freely.
2. Be very careful when you drill the small hole for the propeller wire—it need only be 5 mm in diameter.
3. A bit of cooking oil on the rubber band makes it work better.

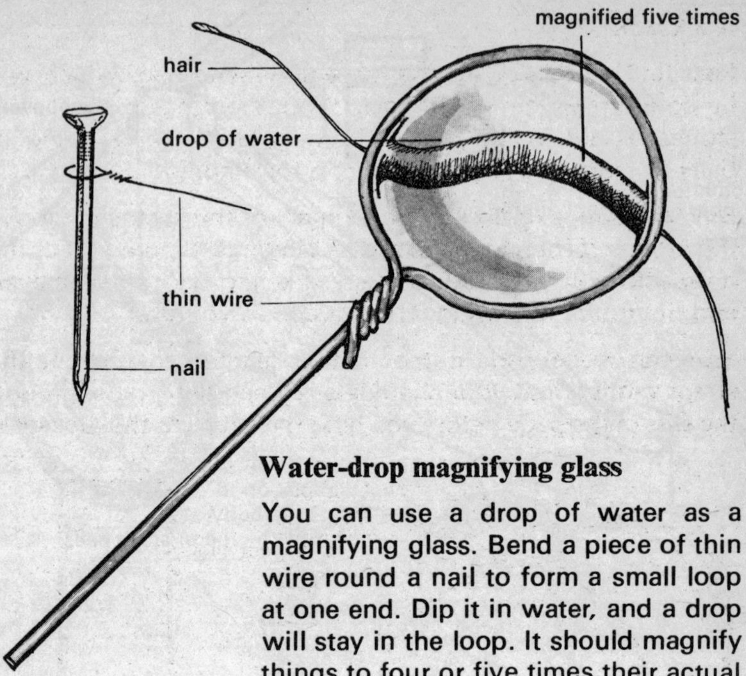

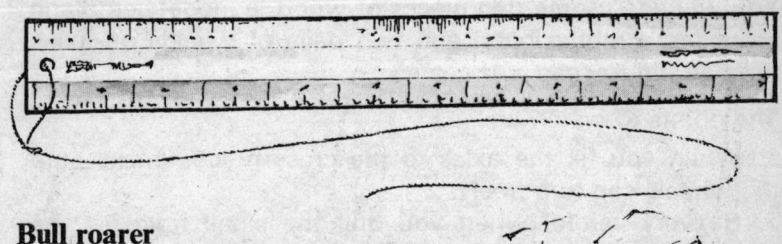

magnified five times
hair
drop of water
thin wire
nail

Water-drop magnifying glass

You can use a drop of water as a magnifying glass. Bend a piece of thin wire round a nail to form a small loop at one end. Dip it in water, and a drop will stay in the loop. It should magnify things to four or five times their actual size.

Bull roarer

This is a thing we always called a bull roarer and all it does is make a noise. It's just a long, flat piece of wood, like a ruler, with a hole in one end. Tie it on to about 60 cm of string and whirl it round your head.

Rucksack

First find a sack, or even a large polythene bag, which will fit comfortably on your back. You then need two small stones to put in the bottom corners, some rope, string or belts to make the straps and string for binding.

Bind the straps to the bottom corners of the sack, just above the stones. (The stones stop the bindings slipping.) Fill the rucksack with your sandwiches, sleeping bag, or whatever, and tie up the top, tying in the straps as you do.

You can make pads out of felt or leather, to prevent the straps cutting into your shoulders. Thread the straps through the slits in the pads before you bind the straps to the rucksack.

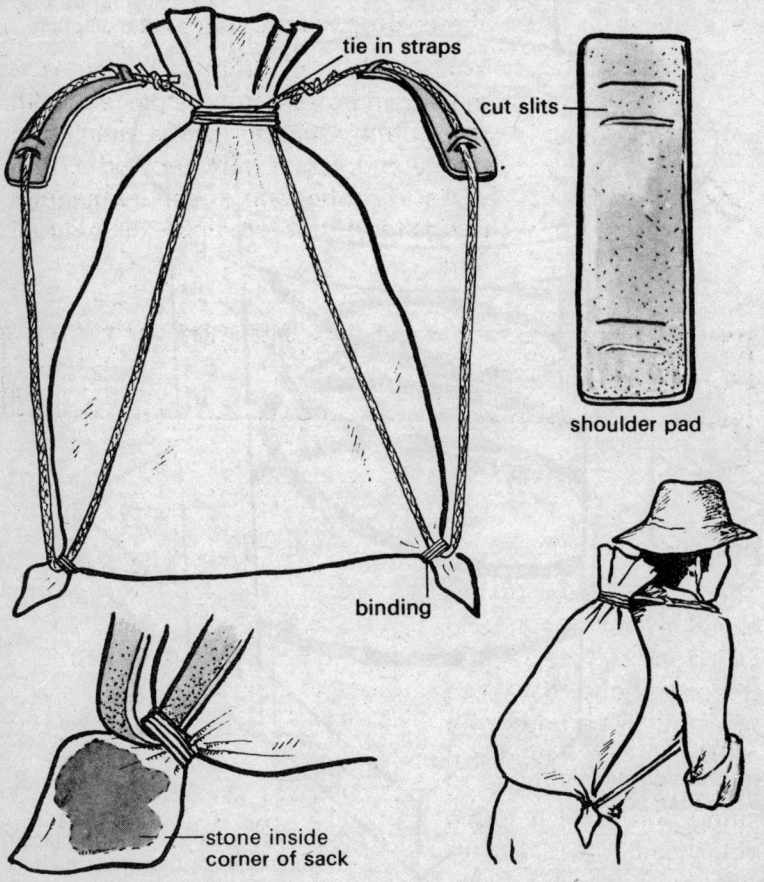

Weighing machine

Here is a machine for weighing heavy or dirty things which you can't weigh on the kitchen scales. You need a strong spring (one from an old mattress or sofa is ideal), a tin plate and five bits of wood.

To mark the scale on one of the side supports, take objects whose weight you already know. Try them on your new weighing machine and mark how far down the plate is pushed. This is called 'calibrating'.

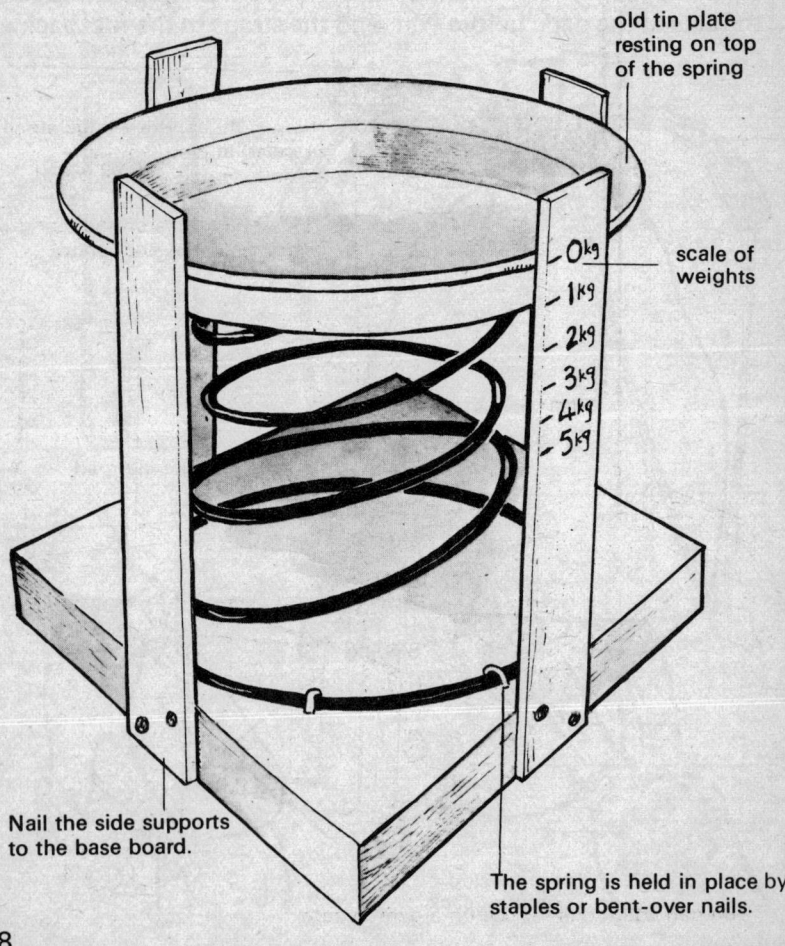

Door closer

Do people always leave doors open in your house? If they do, you can easily make doors shut automatically by rigging up this device.

eye hooks
string

The weight can be a large stone wrapped in cloth so that it doesn't scratch the paintwork.

The weight pulls on the strings, which pulls the door shut.

shelf bracket

You can adapt this for use on a garden gate

Moccasins

Moccasins are a lot easier to make than they look. Ordinary leather is the best material to use, but felt, suede or even old carpet will do.

1. Put your foot on a folded piece of paper, next to the fold, and draw round it.
2. Unfold the paper. Draw and cut round the shape on your material. Draw in the dotted lines.
3. Fold in the middle and sew round the edge with strong thread.
Cut along the dotted lines.
4. Slide your foot in and mark where the heel comes to. Cut away the material ½ cm behind this mark.

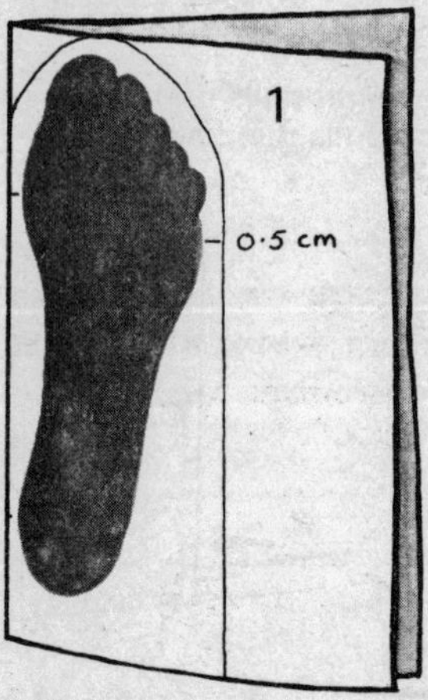

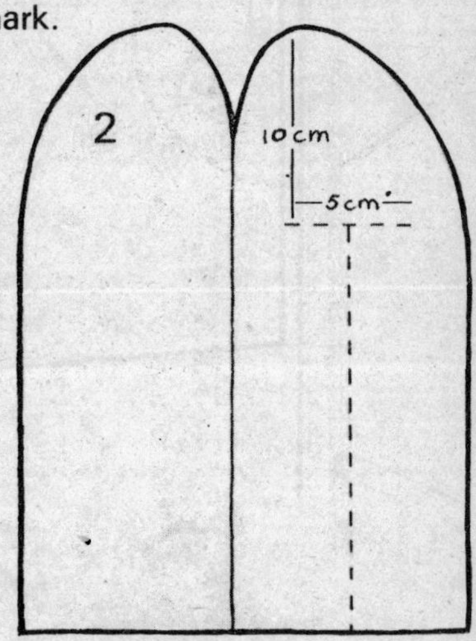

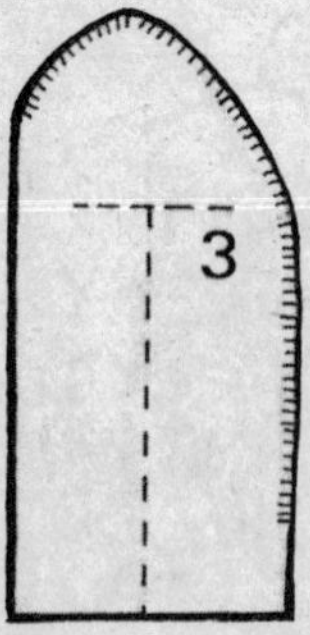

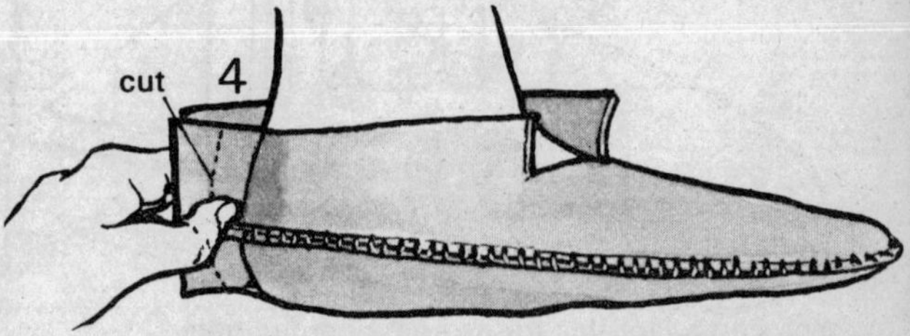

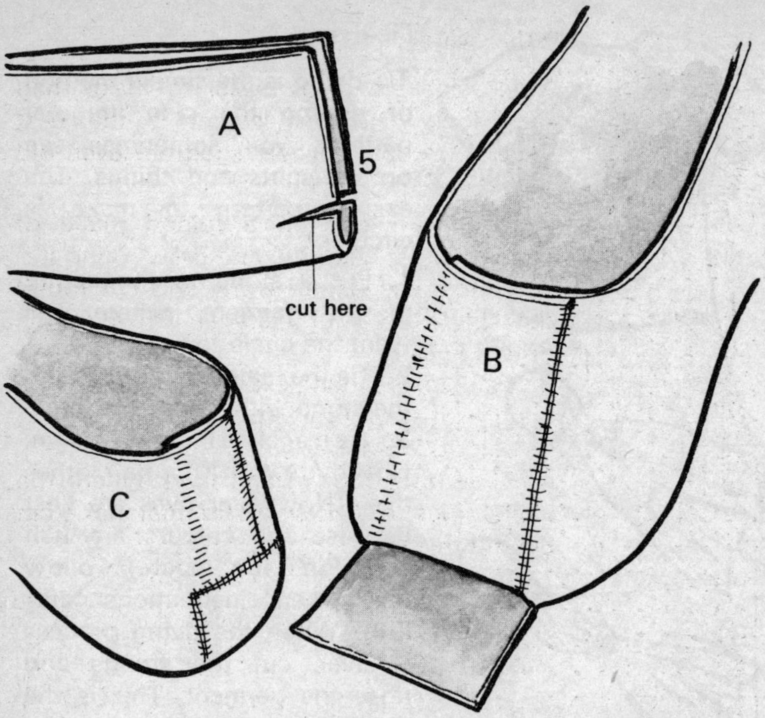

5. Sew up the heel in stages A, B and C.
6. Sew in a tongue 5 cm wide. Fit a lace.
Now make a shoe for the other foot.

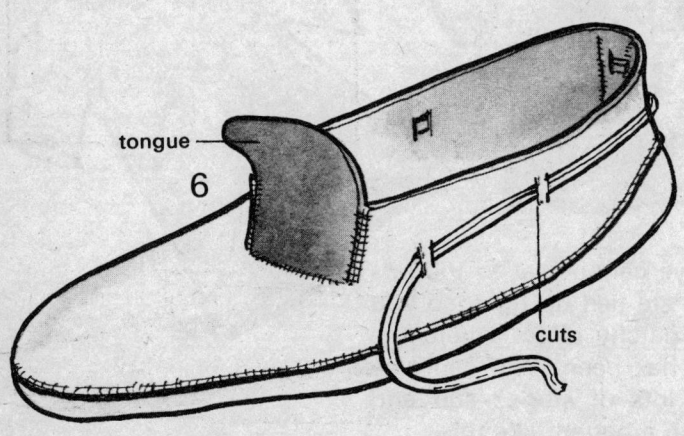

Tie-dying

Tie-dying is the simple method of getting the nice irregular patterns you sometimes see on tee-shirts and things. The easiest pattern to make is circular.

1. Put a stone in the centre of the garment, where you want the circle to be.
2. Tie the material tightly round the stone with string.
3. Tie it again a bit lower down. Now dye it with a normal clothes dye. (Hot water dyes are best because the colours are rich and don't run much.) Follow the makers' instructions carefully. When the dying process is over, cut the strings and rinse the garment. This is the pattern you should have. . .

The dye cannot get to the bits which are tied up tight, so you get a patchy effect where the string has been. You can also tie in lots of stones and end up with a pattern like this. . .

Another type of pattern is irregular stripes.
1. Fold the material in pleats like this...

2. Tie it up tightly and then dye it. It should come out a bit like this...

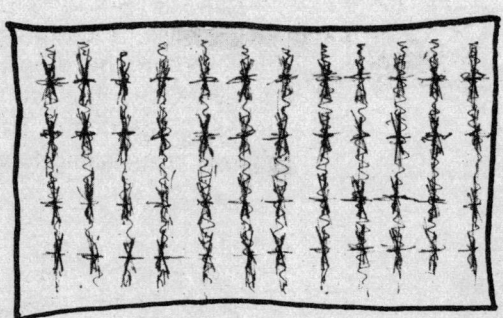

3. If you use combinations of these designs and several different colours, the effect can be amazing.

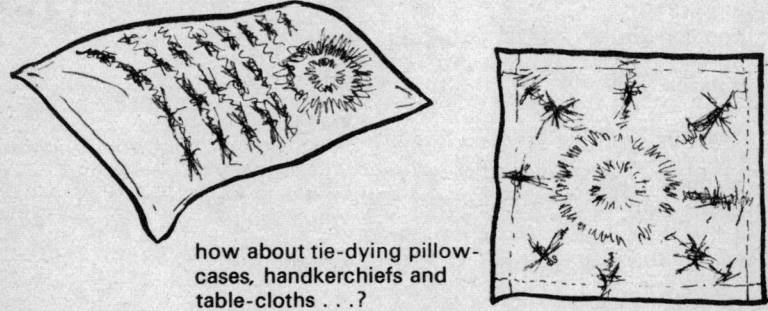

how about tie-dying pillow-cases, handkerchiefs and table-cloths...?

Index

ball, paper 49
balloon, hot-air 30
balsa wood 40, 41
bamboo 22, 28, 29
banjo 44
battery 52
billiards, table-top 37
bivouac 16
boats 38–9
book-box 51
bottles 42
box, cigar 44, 45
bull roarer 56

candle 39, 54
canvas 11, 16, 21
car, propeller 55
cardboard 16, 17, 50
carpet 16, 60
catamaran 40–41
clock, water 26–7
comb 37, 45
cork 23
corrugated iron 17
cotton reel 54

darts, match 36
dens 16–17
door closer 59
dying, tie 62–3

eye hooks 44, 59

feather 15, 23
felt 60
fishing tackle 22–3
foam rubber 11

glider 31
gnomon 25
go-kart 10–11
grenade, water 49

hairgrips 22
hammock 21
hardboard 12
haybox 19

kiln, earth 24
kites 28–9
knots 46

ladder, rope 20
leather pouch 53
leather sucker 53

magnets 52
magnifying glass 56
matchbox 35, 38
matchstick 33, 34, 35, 36, 38, 54
mirror 50
moccasins 60–61
musical instruments 42–3

needle 36

oven 18

pen, quill 15
periscope 50
piano, thumb 45
plaiting 46
planes 32–5
plasticine 31, 33, 34
plywood 12
polythene 16, 17, 28, 29, 57
propeller 32, 33, 55

roller skate 14
rope 20, 21, 46, 47, 57
rucksack 57
ruler 37, 45, 56

safety pin 22
scales 58
shelf bracket 13, 59
skate board 14
sledges 12–13
spring 58
sundials 25

tank, cotton-reel 54
telephone, bush 15
tents 16–17
tissue paper 29, 30
trailer, bike 9

varnish 12, 22

wattle and daub 17
weighing machine 58
wheels, pram 9, 10, 11, 26
whipping 47
whizz bang 48

xylophone 43

yurt 16